Discovering the Divine

Occult Essays

by

Richard K. Page

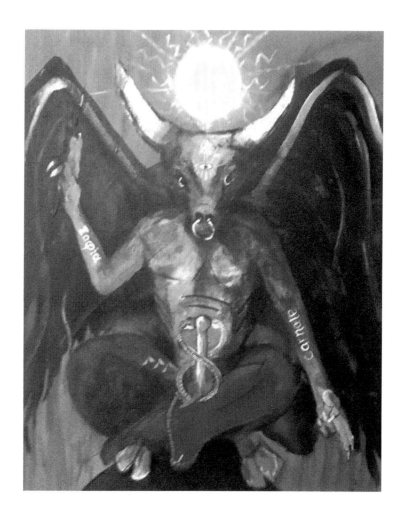

Taurean Sunrise – 2015 Richard K Page

Introduction

Blessed reader, sisters and brothers in the realm of questions. As always, I am unreservedly grateful that you have taken time both now and from your toils to purchase this book; and greater gratitude that you take the time to read it. I shall begin with an apology for merely being a student of these matters, and I will never claim to be a master or an authority, simply a collector of thoughts and evidence for myself to conclude a universe which I call reality. In reading my thoughts all I ask is that you consider them for yourself.

Understand that I will always remain a student of these subjects, and as experience repeatedly tells me, that which I once held as true, carried with the weight of moments that have passed since I last concluded these notion, often that passage of time invalidates previous conclusions. The volume which can be claimed as the summit of my truth can only be determined when it has no potential for change, this is true for all. This concept makes what we call facts and truths transient and subjective to personal realities.

Quite possibly, probably even by the time you read this, I will have written something contradictory that sheds further light on any given topic and this presents new reasoning to me. This is because the search for truth should not end in satisfaction, but further yearning.

My books are an expression of that which I have learned thus far, they are not claims of eternal facts. It is foolish for anyone to claim something as fact in any field. Time and light has always, and without exception raised doubt all of man's claims as a universal truth.

As I said in *Exploring the Divine*, there are no such things as facts, this much I still hold true. I still believe there is much to be learned from my books for those who, like yourselves have inquisitive minds that take joy in the wonderment and questions of existence, it is a noble trait shared by yourself and all the greatest philosophers of all time. The word philosophy means lover of wisdom, not archivist of facts.

I have found favour in the philosophy of Hermetic Gnosticism which underpins the antithetical expression of science. Science, not to be under considered, for the time being, rightly does not concern itself with questions of spirituality. Often people who dedicate themselves to only accepting the measurement of all things in the realm of the material universe dismiss spirituality as immeasurable and that is absolutely a correct stance to take in a doctrine that expresses itself as a measurable quota. We are yet to discover a scientific discipline which can be used to measure the essence of consciousness, love, individuality and reason for existence. As Luciferians, we must not let this restrict our thoughts to match the limitations of science. While the onus of proof lies on the proposer of any subject, the lack of ability to provide physical proof of the existence of such concepts as gods must surely fall to the current level of sciences ability to present this evidence.

Let me put this another way. While it is perfectly rational for a person to reject the idea of any greater spiritual divinity without any physical evidence, we must also accept that there exist conceptual principles that we are not yet at a level of scientific accomplishment to measure things which we know or believe must exist. Love, is one such unquantifiable entity. Although, many may claim they have not experienced love, I believe they are just misrepresenting a concept of love to that of an excessive romantic notion of love. Love simply towards a parent or a child, or someone who has merely passed through a brief period of your life is an emotion which is undeniable. Love quota varies towards other people depending on the extent of that relationship. It exists, I would find it hard to believe anyone who claims they have not experienced love or compassion. Science to date cannot measure love. So, since we must accept that our current level of scientific ability has shortcomings we simply cannot exclude things that science cannot measure as being non-existent.

So, wisdom which concerns itself not with the very quantifiable measures and outcomes that determine science, but with a rational which is more holistic and emotive nature of existence allows for the *sophi*sticated exploration of what is possible

A Sophisticate like yourself, ourselves, must oppose the sedimentary state of established reality, the condition of change is created by our desire for change. All that is called fact will one day be challenged, re-interpreted, re-invented or damn right dismissed as fallacy. The contribution of theory no matter how absurd creates question, and questions lead to truth.

Our search for self and divinity or more importantly the divinity within oneself is often mocked by those who have closed their minds and eyes to anything more than that which is measurable. And by their divine sovereignty they are entitled to stop at that conclusion. I have no will to change anyone's mind on their beliefs. My desire is to explore all possible forms of existence, to ask the big questions like "why are we here?" and to allow a discourse which is not obstructed by those with closed minds. I am currently leaning towards a greater purpose of life and existence, but I'm not going to dismiss the possibility of a chaotic set of random carbon molecules and energy that by happenstance formed consciousness at which we experience our existence. It's a good and perfectly plausible explanation that I cannot disprove. But, equally there are seemingly an endless supply of other theories that I cannot disprove, including a great spaghetti monster. The seeker of wisdom exercises his wisdom thus far, and that wisdom tells me that there is more to life, to consciousness and to me. I'm not one hundred percent sure on what that is and so I read about religion, faith, physics, biology and chemistry. And by exploring all these I can only achieve a personal version of what reality is. Other people's experience is a determining factor on that.

I write these books to share my personal thoughts of what I have found or proposed. I cannot help but feel that people who dedicate themselves to a single discipline even at the highest level of this dichotomous fallacy which proposes that you must choose science or faith and then spend endless hours trying to convince someone else to conform to their ideals. No, dedicate yourself to neither, consider both. Both is the logical decision claiming that the earth is six thousand years old because the bible says so is and ridiculous as deciding that cannot be love because we cannot measure it we all have a degree of scientific mind, we all have a degree of spiritual minds. Gnosticism primary tenet is a parody of that dichotomy. Man is made of two parts, his physical self this is quantifiable in scientific measurement and his spiritual self, which is not. This is as above, the universe has a spiritual essence and a physical one, so is below.

Your reality is all. And I mean it "all", you are the centre of the universe, all things subjectively orbit you and the light that emits from you. Your universal domain is the extent of that reach, all other universes exist within the subjective mind of others, therefore you are the physical manifestation of a God. Do not read that lightly as new age, positive reinforcement gibberish. You need to accept the perspective of your universe, you cannot escape being the centre of it, wherever you go the universe will expand outwardly from your centre of consciousness. Your consciousness is continuously receiving and emitting information which seemingly has no purpose other than to affect your disposition and to influence and be influenced by other sentients around you. Beyond that all is irrelevant unless again you attribute greater relevance to it. So, with that in mind, what does that make you? It makes you God of that dominion. If at any point, you lose sight of that fundamental belief, then you enslave yourself.

The second apology is more material in nature, that this book will be printed in black and white like *Exploring the Divine*, you really would benefit from the imagery in colour, however the current printing method through the publisher allows only full colour printing on every page whether it needs it or not or black and white. This means you pay for a full colour page, whether it needs it or not, this increases the printing costs exponentially, which, really doesn't bother me, it just increases the cost to you. I do not wish to do that. Open your heart and mind, read, conclude and move on.

If you have questions, I can be found quite easily on the internet, feel free to talk. I encourage you to join the Facebook Group 'The Luciferian' where I can be found along with others who will love to share thoughts and insight with, regardless of your particular current state of spiritual passage.

Contents

Introduction to Kybalion Hermeticism.

If you are familiar with the works alleged to have been written by the characters 'The three initiates", then you will be familiar with many of concepts of Gnosticism that I have been sharing. I often refer to a "Collective consciousness" as my version of a God figure, and that I have found is astonishingly similar to "The All within the All", so these teachings when I discovered them heavily influence me as conclusions I had reached seemed to be resonate in pre-existing philosophies, not just those which we are exposed to in our personal worlds, but one that independently produces itself in others, throughout man's history. How often have you conceived a notion only to find out that what you thought was a purely inspired novel idea, others had also concluded. When this happens to me, as it often does, I am left with a mixed emotion of finding myself elated that this concept is already an established reality for some, thus reaffirming my belief in it, but also egotistically disappointed that I thought I had some moment of genius revelation to share, that I can no longer claim sole credit for. Such was the Kybalion, and I have stated in the past "That which is profound, is only somebody else saying that which deep down you already knew was true". Sometimes it takes someone like Oscar Wilde to state the obvious in a way so that the obvious seems revolutionary. I don't want you to think that is in any way some fool like myself diminishing the genius of Wilde, I could only dream of being able to express myself with his wit and ability.

I must confess upon reading the Kybalion it seemingly was a reflection of almost all I come to believe. Some of the things resounded with me very much, and I do recommend that everyone reads it. It is now in the public domain, you can find it with a simple internet search, although a paperback version is available online also for under $5(£4) and for that amount of money I do not think you could buy a better value occult book and that includes anything I have ever written. It's incredibly concise, but profound in that seed of wisdom.

Hermes Trismegistus is a mythological author and philosopher behind the hermetic texts known as the Hermetic Corpus, which presents a syncretic source of all modern-day religions. The book the Kybalion is proposed to be a modern interpretation of the teachings of Hermes Trismegistus.

The Kybalion identifies seven tenets which form the overall ideal of Hermetic wisdom.

1. Mentalism
2. Correspondence
3. Vibration
4. Polarity
5. Rhythm
6. Cause & Effect
7. Gender

Most of which I have covered in my previous writings with similar chapter titles. The Kybalion was first published in the early twentieth century and heavily influenced the then developing *Theosophical Society*. I do also recommend you take an interest in this movement. Some, I will be the first to admit is heavily laced with the Victorian fad of spiritualism in its most obscene sense, but much, oh so-so much is a pure joy of insightfulness.

The following sections review the basic principles of the Kybalion which I have rephrased in my usual layman's version of Luciferian principles. I have endeavoured to Apply this gnosis into a Luciferians self-empowering version of expression.

The Principle of Mentalism.

All is mind. Everything you experience is a presentation towards, or a projection from, your mind. I opened this book with an affirmation that you are the centre of your subjective universe, expanding and reinforcing that, you are by every definition God.

In the known verifiable history of mankind, we have no direct experience of any superior being through-out the universe than mankind himself.

You create your universe. Your subjective universe is the premier universe within your ability to regulate, no other concedes to your divine will more readily.

Thus, you are the facilitator of your personal subjective will, any state of existence that you have experienced that is contrary to your will, is a result of your lack of expression of that will. This could be that you have not taken action to change things sufficiently to match your will at all, you have not taken enough concern in the events to express your will, or that you have not empowered yourself to enact that expression of will.

All other people are equally blessed as Gods of their universe, so therefore others share this law, this means you may find yourself subject to their wilful reality. Adapt the state accordingly.

Will is the persistent determination to impose your law over other laws, all have equal choice to lead or to follow. Choose wisely, being master isn't always the best choice, although it often returns greater dividends, sometimes the carcass of a kill is better eating than the kill.

In life, we experience that the essence of human reason that surmounts to the personality which is the internal "you" resides within an object of physical propensity, your physical vehicle, your body; your body in turn exists within a greater, larger contained organism which we call the Earth. The Earth's physical self-determines the physical laws which we must always seek to overcome. This expression of personal laws over physical laws is an expression of mankind's drive towards his collective apotheosis.

Energy and Matter are comparable with a symbiotic pairing. The mind is our divine mastery of the actions of energy and its counterpart matter. Thought creates the actions of both energy and therefore matter; therefore, all is mind.

We are a physical manifestation of our minds; our minds are one with *The All*. It is within our minds that we live and move and experience all, *The All*.

You age, because you believe that aging is a process that your body must do under universal law, disbelieve it. You suffer, because something causes you to believe that you should suffer, disbelieve it. You have weight issues, because you believe you have weight issues. Disbelieve it. Master your mind and you will master your energy and therefore your matter. But do not think this is simply a matter of wishing and willing, you have to change your environment to match that which you wish to become.

When you were young and growing, you associated with those who were young and growing, and so the laws of development were established to you by collective experience. If you willed to become a doctor, you associate with others who willed to become a doctor in universities and colleges, the influence to create that reality is as much by association to that environment as to the study the environment provided. If you wish to become an actor, hang around with actors. If you associate with thieves and drug users, you enable that aspect of reality as a natural experience of your own universe. Willing change requires that you immerse yourself into that arena so that all you perceive leads to that outcome. We age and die because we allow the universe to dictate this relationship so that as you age, you associate within that age group who ultimately collectively age, decay, become ill and die.

Grasp the laws of the mental universe, own them, be prepared to be responsible for the creation of your will through indifference. You have been guilty of indifference and allowing the will of others to form your state.

The key to will is the known as the *Key of Solomon*. You have always held the key.

> "He who grasps the truth of the mental nature of the Universe is well advanced on the path to mastery."

I'm sure we have all claimed at some point that "This universe is mental!".

This off the cuff remark, also has a deeper more significant esoteric truth behind it. The concept of mentalism at the time suggests that *The All* and by "all" I literally mean a universal all which includes, the universe, you and I, even our thoughts are within the thoughts of the unknowable God *(The All)*. We are effectively *"The All's"* the collective imagination. I have suggested similar, but rather than being "His" imagination, I suggest that our physical universe and its vast separation between stars and planets are a macrocosmic imitation of the atoms in our bodies.

The Kybalion suggest that we are as characters in the book of a great author, I understand that however, it is my premise that rather than being subservient to the will of the great author, we are an individually realised component of that author.

As an author of fictional stories, every character in those stories is an aspect of myself, his thoughts are my thoughts, it is not that I create him, more that he exists within myself.

Similarly, the authors of *The Kybalion* who name themselves as *The Three Initiates* compare this to the works of Dickens and of Shakespeare, or any other literary author for that matter.

They argue well, how the characters within their environments exist further within their own context alone; their implied will is derived exclusively from within the mind of the author, this is an allegoric description of a monotheistic God figurehead.

The three initiates description I suspect was pandering to a Victorian world where blasphemy is still a serious violation of moral aptitude and as controversial as *The Kybalion* was, it still subscribed to a higher master being, separate from the self will of the individual, although I suspect that the Initiates themselves, conceded this point against their otherwise sound logic.

This *great author*, or call him architect if you are of a masonic inclination, is presented as a one directional authority character responsible for all creativity and mastery of all things, I disagree.

The notion of this master god, is contrary to the modern Luciferian philosophy. I am not by any means an atheist, as a theist, but I am not a subject of God I am a part of that God, certainly not abstract to it.

I believe that the characters I create in fiction are fantasy aspects of the pure self. They are expressed with the freedom of a universe designed to allow consequence of will in the way the author believes fitting, we then design a story based upon the friction of these personal universes and self-conflict. The characters with my inspiration eventually become the masters of the outcome by their projected will.

The Kybalion says that "if for example the character Hamlet was to claim that 'I am Shakespeare' then this would-be nonsense". The whole of the character of Hamlet is a contained entity within Shakespeare's mind. And therefore, is unable to know anything beyond the knowledge of that which Shakespeare imbues him with. Indeed, Shakespeare himself in reality claims…

"All the world's a stage, and all the men and women merely players; They have their exits and their entrances, and one man in his time plays many parts, His acts being seven ages".

This fits in nicely with the Kybalion's claims, and I do see where this concept has significance. Unfortunately for us Luciferians the Kybalion is critical of people who claim to be "God" and submits a deference to this greater unknowable force. For this much, I disagree.

Hamlet is more a part of Shakespeare than any man or woman who has ever walked this earth and being a part of something, makes you that something. Anything existing as a component part of any unit or body, becomes that body. Think of Shakespeare, few know the man, all know the work. Hamlet is therefore the id Shakespeare expressed as the ego of Hamlet, yet the true self is the id.

I have created characters, each one of those characters no matter how extreme in nature and unlike me, they are me, in when I put them in the universe I have created in my mind they act as myself in this fantastical reality.

I do absolutely endorse its principle however, because the concept of mentalism, combined with the other six principles do collate into a body of work that forms a foundation of a creative reality in which you can become master of your universe. That alone is a very Luciferian trait.

Hamlet, as the creation of Shakespeare can indeed claim to be Shakespeare, because although the parameters that Shakespeare has applied to the character and his worlds, exist entirely within the mind of Shakespeare, and that Shakespeare while writing the words of Hamlet puts himself into that scenario, and he is unbound in his manifest power to express where Hamlet begins and ends. Hamlet in return, in his artificial lifespan would've formed a living dialogue with Shakespeare. Hamlets life span was a transcendental time within the universe of Shakespeare's head. Believe me, Hamlet lived, maybe not quite as we do, but on an alternative level, and he certainly would have expressed himself to Shakespeare, anything capable of expression is a sentient consciousness in its own right. Every character Shakespeare ever wrote, was an aspect of Shakespeare expressing himself.

The Kybalion considers the All to be infinite in capacity, this was quite revealing to me it its explanation, as I have often considered the universe and its dimensions.

In fact, the ponderance of the universe was the opening passage of a previous book, how unfathomable the size is and the boundaries which my isolated mind must conceive an outer objective view of all things since I am contained within something which is unfathomable to be viewed from an observational external perspective.

What is explained is that of the capacity of *The All's* mind is a reflection of the capacity of our own mind, where we have seemingly infinite learning capability and to absorb the imagination of a principle does not require an expansion of the physical size of the brain to accommodate.

The Kybalion, much like Qabalah which I believe title is intended to create association with, suggests that to manifest things, all things must first form in the mind as a formative pre-stage. *The Key* to manifestation of desire comes from being able to tap into the energies and vibrations of the experienced universe. And that the laws of our reality are the *All-within-All's* unchangeable laws, and while it is impossible to defy these laws, we can use greater laws against weaker ones if we study the laws and their relationships, physical and metaphysical.

This brings us nicely onto the second tenet of the Kybalion, that of Correspondence.

The Principle of Correspondence

There is a relationship that exists between laws, actions and states of all things. All things are subject to laws by what I would term a divine hierarchy, cause and effect. Yet the first law we learn in life is that our minds can affect change in states. We think to move our fingers, and our fingers move. There is a physical relationship between our minds and our immediate vessels, our bodies. We desire food and with our first primal scream we shape the air that surrounds us causing it to vibrate and our first command is issued to another abstract mind, who then proceeds as instructed to feed us, a rudimentary and subjective language is formed, even before we subject ourselves to the existing rules of our geographical language environment.

Ask and you shall receive.

Learn how to affect change around you. Seasoned masters instruct others to manipulate the physical world. As the pharaoh instructed thousands of nameless men to build the pyramids. Pharaoh's will was met, and the pharaoh's names as magister of this great fete became the creators without laying a single stone. Their name was eternalised. Architects of their environment, the pyramids bear the names of the masters not of the servants. Mastery of others begins with mastery of self, do not think for one moment that authority comes from a badge or uniform, it comes from within, and attempts to force authority without inner mastery will always result in contempt and resistance from those you attempt to master.

Nothing great is achieved by one alone, yet one alone, using his mind efficiently a person can bring great change to all around. Learn how to shape the universe around you and allow the momentum of this force, to resonate through others.

Understand the self, and you shall understand all. Do not find yourself bewildered by those who seek to obfuscate the simplicity of the laws of correspondence. Nothing is complicated, until somebody desires to obfuscate it and claim mastery. The fraudulent man often places premiums based upon him hiding the simplicity of things, and convincing you to trust the work to him. In learning skills, traits and knowledge. If you fail to understand something that you passionately seek knowledge on, then the failure most likely lies with the expert in his explanation. Find another expert.

Correspondence forms the principle that there exists a hierarchical law of relationships which utilises the "As Above, So Below" stalwart of gnostic mantra's. One which I wholeheartedly subscribe to in many different interpretations. Never is so much revealed with so few words as "As Above, So Below", it presents itself in all manner of occult concepts that it truly is the most profound statement ever written.

The laws all answer to a greater and more powerful law, yet one law residing deep within another may find itself master of a superior law. Almost exhibiting itself like a game of Rock, Paper, Scissors. An example has already been given above where the character Hamlet is contained within the mind of Shakespeare, and therefore he falls under the laws of the world Shakespeare allotted to him, likewise Shakespeare himself is within the mind of *The All* which is again, within *The All,* yet within the mind of Shakespeare the universal laws of nature can be eradicated for the laws of nature which Hamlet must concede.

The hierarchical planes of correspondence form a harmonic layered model between three "Greater" planes of experience, Physical, Mental and Spiritual which in Hermetic Gnosticism form the archetypal *Holy Trinity*.

I think the important part of the Kybalion's explanation of the principles of correspondence lies in its description of the interoperation of the planes. Which are often perceived as a linear level of progression, whereas in fact they are closer to aspects, dimensions or states of existence, and much like our three-dimensional physical universe a precise condition of any one thing is an amalgamation of its states within multiple dimensions.

For example, to define a ping pong ball in a square room there are many dimensions that could define its state, each one providing more and more detail towards the absolute truth-state.

Simplest we have its geomatical X, Y & Z co-ordinates, each representing a physical locational dimension. We could add *Time* as a fourth dimension to give a mathematical and precise position of where that ball is at any given moment. Other states could include, its colour, size, mass and shape we assume spheroid, but it may be a dented ball so possibly giving it multiple locations on an atomic level.

The Kybalion questions what states define a plane over a dimension or a state and gives an extremely good explanation.

The Principle of Vibration.

ALL is in motion, always. From the atomic to the cosmic, all is constantly moving, all is excited, all vibrates. The shape of the atom, mirrors the shape of the cosmos. And so once again…

> *That which is within, is without. That which is above, so is below.*

Nothing is at rest. The rates of vibration determine that which is manifest. Be it the spectral luminance of light reflected from that which we believe is physical, to the density of lead. Its vibrations determine how it manifest itself in our universe. Sound, light and even physical force which equates to its material existence are all expressions of a vibration.

High vibrations are akin to mind, lower vibrations are akin to light, yet further lower vibrations are akin to sound, and even lower vibrations are akin to air, lower vibrations are akin to water, further lower vibrations are akin to stone. This spectrum of vibrations forms all things. We exist as a receptor of vibrational occurrence.

The laws of correspondence determine the method one can use towards manipulation of the laws of vibration.

> Every grain of sand that forms, contains the entire universe, frozen in a moment of time. That which is formed is unchangeable, and is as past. That which is forming in the mind is the future. It shall come to pass and become as dust.

Louis de Broglie, 1892-1987 wrote his PhD describing the wave nature of electrons and suggested that all matter had wave properties, waves are a resultant motion of vibrations. De Broglie won the Nobel Prize for Physics in 1929, after the wave-like behaviour of matter was first experimentally demonstrated in 1927. It concluded that light contains particles, tiny concentrations of pure energy, these become incorporated into the wave because of vibrations and this suggests that all particles, like the electron, must be transported by a wave into which it is incorporated. De Broglie later was instrumental in the shaping of the new wildly accepted *De Broglie–Bohm theory,* also known as "The pilot wave theory".

These discoveries and theories still being pondered today, are contained in the Kybalion and Hermetic Gnosis written thousands of years ago.

The use of vibration is to change one's mental state, in the same way we create vibrational change in our voice which carry command to others, we in turn can alter the vibrational states of our consciousness, effecting physical change in our surroundings, because any vibration interacts with the state of other artefacts around them.

If you place our ping-pong ball in a bowl of water, then you cause vibrations in the water, the ball is affected. Since all things vibrate, the master of vibration causes harmony when multiple things around it resonate at the same rate.

This is a foundation for achieving what people would call "special" or "magical" powers. We demonstrate it regularly in our lives with what we term "natural" abilities, such as speaking. We've mastered that, but that is not the extent of our manipulation of vibration, it is up to us to discover new ways of doing so affecting atomic change.

If you have ever been dancing, that is an example of the power of vibration, dancing often leads to relationships, why? Because the sound creates resonance, we react and harmonise our entire bodies to the rhythm of the music. Furthermore, when we become familiar with a song, we will probably join in the singing of it, our minds become only the song, our bodies move to the rhythmic beats of the song. And we find an affiliation with those sharing this resonance, other dancers. Therefore dance, and music even ritualistic chants are often used as part of magical ceremony. The purpose of using music in this way is to align localised vibrations to a common cause.

The Principle of Polarity

Everything has two poles. Thesis and antithesis are identical in nature, but different in degree. Often things which we call opposites are the same thing, differing only in degree of self-expression. The pairs of what we often call opposites can always be reconciled, extremes meet, everything is and isn't at the same time. All truths are but half-truths, every truth is half-false, there are two sides to everything.

To explain the common misconception that which we believe to be opposite are in fact degrees of expression of the same thing. The head of a coin, still a coin when compared to the tail.

Hot is as cold, just a different degree of temperature in relation to its greater environment. The temperature is as the spectrum of light, it is a law subject to the law of vibration.

Identifying the laws that apply to any point of the scale between polarities, will return the laws that apply to every point in the scale between the polarities.

Consider Polarities before determining outcome and actions. You may exist on one side of a coin, be foolish and reject your polar adversary, or be wise and realise that the coin "as a whole" is wherein the value lies.

This is a simile of love and hate, the principle of God and Satan as abstract opposites is wrong, they are unified opposites. The adversary is "he who is not us", yet we are multifaceted in all aspects, so there exists within both God and The Devil an adversary from their subjective positions. If Satan means the adversary, then Jehovah is actual a Satan to the devil and so our subjective and personal adversaries are not opposition but oppositional.

He, is our equal and our opponent. Our mastery and energy is lost while we waste time battling a perceived adversary who for all other intents and purposes are really just like us. Look to creating both ideals, not compromise. Compromise is always shared disappointment. Achieve this and you will always be master.

Transmute Lead into Gold.

This ancient concept is very much in agreement with the scientific relationships of vibrations. Hermeticism and quantum states return the principles of polarity, where in the principles presented in the reality of the state of *Schrodinger's Cat*, or *Young's experiment* things both exist, and don't exist at the same time. And the state is determined only by observation.

This is significant to us occultists, very significant. Science confirms on our behalves that reality really is only created by observation of the conscious mind and that furthermore since all observation is subjective to an individual, when one individual observes it, it fixates that state for all time.

The principle of Mentalism is supported by current scientific research.

Quantum mechanics is the new frontier of man's understanding of existence from scientific terms. It is at a point where the very fabric of what we call *fact* acts as bubble that hides the outer realms of the unknown and the occult, where observable science ends and what lies beyond can and always will be purely speculation. Quantum physics is what the world's best and renowned scientists have pondered and debated for over one hundred years, but still their conclusions verge into the esoteric concepts laid out as the foundation stones of many religions going back to the dawn of recorded history around six thousand years ago, who's spoken word goes back an unknowable distance.

It appears to me that we have gone full ourobiatic circle in some of the basic concepts of nature and so now we find ourselves identifying a correlation between esoteric knowledge held by the wizards and philosophers in the times of pre-history to the newly discovered building blocks of reality in the scientific community. For years and still to this day we were told we were nut-jobs and kooks, and more by those who instead of questioning to the nth degree as we, were content to regurgitate the declared reality of those who simply had contemporary platform. Once more we claim our place as magisters of wisdom, knowledge and science.

The state in between which we have been a part of increasingly is looking like human failing to understand correctly the knowledge long since held and forgotten by our ancestors, and in our foolishness instead of correctly dispersing these simple fundamental concepts in a way that makes it clear what they are about, we have disguised them in parables and religious mythologies. We have assigned them names and personas and aligned them with what we call a deific significance instead of aspects of concepts. The result we share todays is a unity of man in a belief of a mythical concept originating from misunderstood philosophy or science.

We are too quick to blame our distant ancestors for the creation of our modern and limiting religious. Whereas, in truth, the real culprits are only a few generations old are very modern and evolved men.

The Golden Era of man exploded between ten-thousand and four-thousand BC (BCE if your insistent on separating a measurement on time with any relation to a religious concept, to me surely the important thing is the measurement, I'm not trying to make an anti-Christian point here, there's plenty of other more important things to make that point on). This occurred somewhere in between then and now when we strayed from a very enlightened and philosophically wise society which paved the way for the pioneer great Greek philosophers, into a modern world of rules which dictate morality based on the judgement of others and their precept judgement of their particular chosen God figurehead. Seemingly at some point some madman decided that pious fetishes of inflicting a greater connection to god than our neighbours were simply based on how immorally we can stand in judgment against others and their morality.

Quantum states, trying not to drift off the comparative philosophies, is currently dominated by one perplexing question. The shape of light?

Light as we study it was often thought to operate similarly to sound, a radial wave traveling outwardly from a central source. I am certain at some point growing-up, that you will regularly have heard the term "light-waves" to describe the shape of light in motion.

While we often make use of light as a tool and we know of many ways extract energy from its source in the form of light; thermally for example. We have even have learned to break light up into its component "wave"-lengths. It is length of wave within light dictates its place in our visible spectrum, its colour. First documented by Sir Isaac Newton and shared through his public lectures in 1669, Newton proposed the controversial idea that light was not a wave but a particle, this was contrary to the then widely accepted work by Rene Descartes.

The simple difference which is purely to ensure that we are all on a level playing field here is - that waves, like ripples expanding from a stone thrown into a pond disperse their energy equally in all available directions unless they meet resistance. Particles on the other hand are single micro bits of energy traveling in a single direction also until it hits something or interacts with something such as the medium it is traveling through. Newton did not invent the prism, but he is forever entrenched in its use that we have all used to replicate his division of light into its constituent colours.

A quick pop quiz for you before reading on. How many colours is light broken up into by the spectrum? Seven you may well think. Well right there is another piece of religious influence on this topic, seven is not at all the number of colours produced by this experiment. The correct answer is an infinite number. But that is the third time Seven has been mentioned with unsubstantiated authority so far in this book, due to its influence on beliefs both spiritual and scientific.

In our current concern, seven is not even a distinct measure of hues based on human perception, in fact our perception is limited to only three, another number which has great esoteric correlation.

Seven, in the case of our perception of the spectrum was chosen for the same reason we believe the earth was built in seven days, why we measure our week by those same seven days, the seven deadly sins, the seven virtues, it is why we have the Seven sisters of the Pleiades constellation and a heptagram (Septagram) is considered an ancient and arcane symbol, the seven visible planets that form our gods and deities, even this presentation on the Kybalion has seven tenets, and Shakespeare's acts of man, which are seven in ages.

Septagram is taken from the 'sept' linguistically forms the number seven, if you imagine two lines 'inter-sept' they could be shown as a right angle ┐ or a 7 and "gram" is Greek origin meaning line, intercepting-lines, give the intercepting lines seven in number and we arrive at a Septagram.

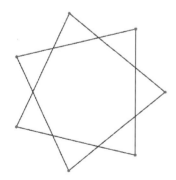

The star formation it creates is based on its point of origin skipping alternate points six times till it returns to its own origin in two-dimensional space.

It also skips past its origin on the fifth transition, this fifth transition is replicated in our working week where we normally work for five days, leaving two which were originally dedicated to god.

With some astrological significance to the order of things, the day of the sun (Sunday) and the primary star in our solar system (the Sun) are to be considered primary principles in many of the multi layered concepts laid out in hermetic gnosis.

The universe is infinite in its capacity, but it is also a system that hosts its own personal polarity. It, despite its infinity is a closed system defined within that infinity. Therefore, the flow of energy that exists within that closed circuit does not act the way our closed electrical circuits act, basic electrical circuits allow the current to pass from positive to negative on a two dimensional board following the path of least resistance. It is by introducing resistance at certain points in the board we can make it do things that result in our wonderful technology. The universe however finds its points of least resistance at seemingly random points in our three-dimensional universe.

One of the ways we commonly experience these points is by their formation of what we call gravity. I cover this idea later in the book.

The Principle of Cause and Effect.

Every action has an equal action reflecting its state in the scale of polarity.

Everything happens as a resultant combination of the effects of hierarchical laws. Master those laws and you master all things that collimate in an effect.

Those effects create new causes for further effects.

Be aware of the effects of your effects. Combine causes to create specific effects.

Observing effects and knowing that which they in turn cause, allow you to predict future events.

Place yourself above the dichotomy of cause and effect, master that which affects you and become cause.

Cause begins with will.

You may well have heard of the principles of cause and effect from early years of science in school, it is an accepted principle in physics. However, in physics studies you were probably only exposed to the very restricted ideals of such principles within the boundaries of scientific study. You were probably never told how to use this concept in everyday actions. In your chemistry class, you may have lit a Bunsen burner under a liquid the liquid heats due to the flame, it turns into a gas. This is a cause and effect. It may have been explained by the popular principle "Every action has an equal and opposite reaction" which forms Newtons third law.

In life, even every thought you have works towards shaping your idea of existence. Contemplation of cause and effect is an ideal topic to focus on when spending time meditating. Because the principle clearly works both ways, every effect you see had a cause. When trying to contemplate the obstacles, issues or preferentially goals in your life it helps to analyse each topic independently in the remit of cause and effect. Assuming you are familiar with meditation techniques the, early stages will often present you with what I would call the clear head. It is at this point during meditation that practitioners will introduce the goal of the meditation, this can be hypnosis treatments, lucid dreaming or astral projection. However, when self-practicing at the point of the clear head you should introduce the issues in your life that you want to improve or eradicate. Imagine the issue as a circular object floating is space above it is "its" future, below it is the past. I suggest that you perceive the above as "its" future as the issue you seek resolution to may be a goal in the future, like being a rock star. That goal is not now, it is already a future event. Likewise, an issue from the past may have already had subsequent events. So, the issue must be independent of the current time.

When looking for causes to events draw a line downwards in your imagination and create another circle at the end, write in or imagine that cause as a moment. You may find that your issue or even its legs may have more than one part, however you must analyse all the collective causes that lead to that effect, likewise you must see that effect as causality to a future event, an ideal outcome maybe. This clear isolation of an event in your life can help to repair issues you are currently facing by analysing specific events that collective brought you to this outcome.

The Principle of Gender

Gender is the manifestation of polarity. All things express gender and all that is created is a result of the union of these polarities.

All that is destructive, creates and all that creates must destroy under the law of cause and effect.

The path of follows the pattern of generation, regeneration and creation, within each gender exists sub-genders, within each sub-gender exists further sub-genders, ad-infinitum. All that is created is manifest with its primary gender.

To serve your primary gender exclusively is to neglect the principle of polarity. The hermetic principle of gender while linked to polarity directs us more towards the idea of progression, change and re-manifestation on a metaphysical level. It explains the interoperation between the polarities. The polarities as explained operate on a spectrum of state, where that which we call opposition is in-fact the same thing yet on opposing ends of the spectrum.

Gender however is more to do with relational expression, it is through gender that these articles are able to interact with each other and also continue their eternal expression of change. Trying initially to avoid the obvious explanation of sexual intercourse to present a description of this principle, I would like to present another way to show how this force is present in all things.

When you heat water in a pan, the fire below interacts with the water, its opposing element, through the rising heat. Heat is the masculine expression of gender operation in this case.

The heat is the article, rather than the fire or the water which are the participants. The transference of state is enabled by expressions of gender at this moment of the fire, take note of the "at this moment" as the fire will not remain masculine in all cases.

In sex, it is because of gender that we are able to essentially live forever, not in a conscious subjectiveness, but in the essence of the stream of life that exists within you. It requires a conduit to travel and that conduit is often opposing your current state.

The well-known Yin-Yang symbol is possibly the greatest symbol of gender imaginable. The polarity is expressed by the black and white extremes, but the gender is expressed by the way the polarities within that symbol interact with each other. Both elements of the symbol penetrating each other and both encompassing the penetration of the other. By doing so, they define the whole and create the whole in gender terms one gives and the other receives, equally the recipient gives and the donor receives. There is a feeling of motion within the symbol, a cyclic eternal state of change where if we imagine the yin-yang symbol rotating on its centre point, it intrudes on its counterpart's space, yet in doing so it is penetrated by its counterpart with equal measure. An infinite repetition of creation by destruction and destruction by creation. This constant state of flux is the expression of continuance through change.

There has been a lot of controversy lately regarding gender in terms of the sexual dynamics of humanity. People who search for a very subjective identity feel that the way we express gender in modern life does not reflect their mental gender, and they are correct. The relationship between gender and polarity are so intertwined that in modern, dumbed down society we have somewhat lost the real definition of gender in favour of the simplified polarized aspect of it.

Gender is a spiritual essence in the case of human sexuality. It defines not just your sexual orientation but your capacity to procreate at all, your sexual drive, the kind of people you are attracted to, your potential reproductive ability. But, it doesn't stop there, it is equally responsible for other people's attraction towards you, your masculinity, femininity and receptiveness towards advances. In terms of gender, all people have both masculine and feminine traits. Our sex dictates only our subjective method of reproduction and is an expression of polarity. But our gender is the mechanism that brings that expression into the interaction of others.

All things have gender and contrary to my above statements we do tend to express these genders in a very simplistic male and female dichotomy.

In terms of physical conceptualisation, the feminine aspect is a recipient, and the male aspect is a donor.

The act of eating for example, what you eat is male, the act of eating is female. By continuing this theme, the transfer of energy from that food into your body is akin to the sexual transference of life seed from man to woman.

The modern interpretation of homosexuality being a sin is simply based upon this principle. The idea being that because it causes the cessation of the "seeds" potential to evolve into its next generation of existence by male to male sexual activity. The act is seen by the zealots as not conforming to the potential continuance of life as intended by their God. However, in real terms it is no more a sin than eating food with empty calories, or even more so than throwing out perfectly good food. The sin is simply that the spiritual potential, life potential or energy potential is lost.

When put into those terms, it's kind of ridiculous that people take the whole homosexuality thing as an affront to God. The failure of potential generation is proliferate in nature, and in hermetic principles, since all things are the body of "god" God, being all things is as homosexual as [1]Louis Spence, in fact Louis Spence being as much a part of the holistic god as anyone else, is an expression of God.

An interesting notion that will appeal to Luciferians whose contemplation of ego often comes down to consideration of one's will, is that the "will of self" is male, it is forceful outward expression of the intention of the current state of one's mind. But, what will really help you to reflect on the definition and subtleties of gender is to stop for a moment now, and consider that while the will is male in gender, its counterpart "desire" is female. Will being an intruding donor of expression, whereas desire seemingly so similar, is a recipient of the current state of one's mind, embracing of the minds intention. It's a very difficult thing to distinguish

[1] Louis Spence, a profoundly flamboyant British dancer and entertainer, who is truly fabulous!

between, what counts as will and what counts as desire, the two are almost indistinguishable when applied to a singular self, yet we can perceive them in absolute opposition when we add a second instance of consciousness to the expression.

Gender is simply a push and pull mechanism, it subjectivity provides only the aspectual view of the concept. To explain how the subjectiveness is important consider that:

- Matter becomes fuel.
- Fuel becomes energy.
- Energy becomes matter.

In the first statement matter is the masculine, fuel is the feminine. In the second, fuel becomes the masculine and energy becomes the feminine, and lastly energy is the masculine and matter is the feminine. This is the distinction between gender and sex. We are of a defined sex by our physical attributes, but gender is transitional dependent on state.

Understanding the All within The All

'The All' is all, an organism which is the collective of all physical, mental aspects of the universe, and its relationship with itself no matter how large or how small it is. The individual thoughts and memories that create the mental "you" combines with all the physical matter that is "you". Combined they define you.

Extend that vision with other attributes, your home, your family, your pets. Together they make extended external perceptions of you.

Extend that to your town, and you get the collective you as perceived by people not of your town. Continue to your country, your planet, your solar system, your universe.

All minds in the universe affect the universe in the same way that you moved your fingers as a child. We fist learn to master our immediate physicality, using other forces, such as the sound of our cry we affect things external to our immediate command. Master that, and then extend your command.It is as one humanity we will further our reach across the universe.

Consciousness of man was learned over aeons, it did not start with apes, it started when a single piece of matter affected another and benefited from that change. When that benefit was realised, we learned. The ability to learn is the cause of consciousness. Matter combined and worked as a unit under one consciousness, this formed the first organism. It may have taken billions of years to reach anything we could now call life, but we are descendants of that event.

We mastered the ability to draw stardust from across the universe and command it to form the vessel we call "our body". We then learned to manipulate this matter and shape it into a form which stands upright and dominate the earth on which we stand. We shall continue in the mastery of the material, although we may be on a very low rung of that ladder.

The outpouring of divine energy continues to flow from *The All* into matter under our command. We are God. Be not atheist, for evidence of god is your divine will which began before time under the laws of cause and effect. But neither seek a superior god, it does not exist externally, it is manifest in you, you are a part of a living all, blessed with dominion over the matter you manifest as you and the universe is as you have chosen to perceive it.

The All within The All is the realisation of the divinity of self. What you think is part of a collective thought that shapes your society, collective societies create countries, and so on. A god exists, I assure you. But you are a part of it not external and subservient to it. All religious doctrine state this, but few understand. Read your bible, and hear, God is everywhere, allow him into your heart. Read this as true, and allow THE KNOWLEDGE of who you are into your heart and hold fast. I AM GOD manifest in flesh and blood and I stare at the wonderment that I am, both above and below wherein I exist as a state in that dichotomy.

Ask not why the external god did not help those in need. YOU ARE GOD, intercede if it is your will or sit idly by while children starve and complain that god is impotent, this is expressing the reality that you are impotent. And you create your own reality.

ALLAH means ALL, yet they argue like children over who's all is the real ALL or whose prophet is the real prophet, fools, all is all. It is worthy of note that Allah is not a Muslim God, it's just the word for God in Arabic language, and it has been shared by Jewish and Christian faiths since they began. Its only recently that it has been exclusively aligned to Islamic faiths.

What is Reality?

When explained off the bat, it all sounds like the stuff of science fiction, nobody in their right mind would accept this hypothesis as being a valid explanation of that which we coin 'Reality'. Yet strangely, this hypothesis is as valid as any other we currently have, and thus far in our 4.5 billion years of evolving as a part of the complex unquantifiable biosphere which forms our entire universe, neither religion nor science can rule out as impossible the shortly following premise.

It all comes down to what we know about the deepest nature of reality, and in truth, despite all our investigation and understanding of the complexities of what is presented before us of existence. Existence can only be quantified by a very simple set of rules, these three "Kings" of rules have been long established. Somewhat subliminally, they have been taught in Gnosticism, Christianity, Paganism, Sikhism, in fact you name a faith or religion, you will find somewhere in their legend or dare I say mythology, a recurrence of these grounding principles in this nature.

Modern social evolution is moving away from the oppressive nature of organised religion and many perceive religion is a nonsensical control mechanism for the feeble minded. But I am a man of theosophy, and I have faith in the philosophies and notions of mine, or our ancestors. They were not as superstitious and misconceived as we are determined to make them out to be.

For those of you who are intent to lock yourself in the realms of Science over faith, I'm afraid that this is one of the principles where the material laws of our universe and the philosophies of Religion are in complete accordance.

And if, we can conclude that the root nature of religions share their principles with the root nature of the known sciences, then just maybe the ancient words of man, in stories of what they called gods, were more understanding of science than our contemporary educators give them credit for.

In fact, my opinion, I believe it is more likely that it is we that fail in understanding, as we don't understand what they were trying to tell us about the makeup of reality from a scientific perspective. So, what is this great shared gnosis, that aligns the ancient Gods to modern day scientific laws of physics?

It is as simple as this, what we think a God is today, is not what ancient man thought God was. We have been so indoctrinated with a concept of a nonsensical god figure that we can no longer interpret a reference to a god without metamorphosing it into a character of human attributes, in shape, size and reason.

You see, the basic mechanics of all existence are varying examples of one simple trinity, they are a state of duality or opposition, and an entropy or transference between the two states. That's it. That is the universe, that is all time, that is matter, and all energy, all summed up. All of existence from one corner of the universe to the other, is result of a state of one of those three forms of exhibiting itself. From the moment of creation, be it a principal thought by an all-encompassing God, a designer or grand architect, or a Big Bang where all matter was created as a result of a sudden expansion of energy into an endless void. Both religious and scientific principles conform to this observation.

The "all" presents itself either as matter or as energy. And so, as matter is spent energy is produced, as energy is spent matter is produced and all that we know is a state somewhere between the two and the observational state of transition between these two opponents. These are the "three kings" of principle. These are the "Holy Trinity" A father (original state), a son (the entropic state of change), the holy ghost (the resultant state post transition).

The Original state and the Resultant state form an opposing duality, to simplify try to imagine all things as a proverbial coin. It is heads or it is tails, while up in the air spinning on its axis of undetermined outcome it is the third state which lies in entropy, a transition to the outcome which will be set as one or the other. The coin in the above example isn't exactly the most perfect analogy, but it is the simplest, as while spinning in the air, there is a seemingly chaotic randomness of the outcome which could be either heads or tails, and while there are chaotic outcomes in nature, this is just a result of more complex entropy from other outside forces that determines an outcome on related dualities. When observed to the simplest level, all these entropies follow a specific course, heads will always become tails or tails will always become heads at some point, and the flow between isn't random when all other factors of the universe as a single entity play a part in its resultant state. However, the coin toss mentioned above is influenced by the amount of energy you put in to the toss, the original state it was in before you tossed it, planetary gravity, coin balance and the gentle breeze caused by the wings of a butterfly many miles away. The whole universes state and time affects the outcome of that coin toss, in isolation it is seemingly random, but it is not, because even down to the moment you tossed that coin, an infinite number of events that are miraculous must have occurred to bring about this moment, you and your decision to flip that coin. Think about your ancestors, the fights and struggle they had to exist and to create children just to create you at this moment in time, the fact that life exists on this planet at all which sits at the [2]*Goldilocks zone* orbiting a star that is the true God in ancient definition of this earth, without this benefactor no life would exist. *Chaos or Destiny, a sequence of events must only conclude with only one outcome if all universal factors are taken into account.*

And that is just the first hint that the universe, like a computer program is pre-set. You then add to that, the root comparison to how a computer works. A computer works like this. No matter how complex the envisioned environment may be, in you simulated computer game, how good its graphics are, and the fact that through headphones you can hear the "actual voice" of your friend across the continent. What you see, even what you hear from your friend, is not his real voice and this is not a real world your character is playing in. It is a complex exhibit of a very simplified binary system, a collection of ones, zero's and change is determined by the state between. Your friend's voice, may sound exactly as it does in real life, it may be slightly distorted by the mechanics

---

[2] Our planet occupies what scientists sometimes call the Goldilocks zone. Its distance from our star means it is neither too hot, nor too cold to support liquid water - thought to be a key ingredient for life. Astronomers are searching for rocky planets like ours in the Goldilocks zones of other stars. From google.

of the internet between and amplified by the volume of your TV, but as real as that sounds to you, you are experiencing not your friend's real voice, but a computer simulation of it. You may have dismissed this fact; you may never have known it. But it is sufficient simulation of reality for you to not care to distinguish between it, and actual reality. So this begs the question, how far can we trust all we observe?

How can we say for sure that our eyes show us a full spectrum of colours? We know they do not, the known spectrum of light disappears from the human eye perception and the far ends of Ultra-violet and Infra-red and possibly beyond. What we do know of light is that it is a form of energy that excites receptive nerve endings in our eyes, our eyes absorb this energy and convert it into a data stream that passes through a neural network to be interpreted by our brain as visual imagery. This one form of sensory information forms the mainstay of what we believe is real, to this effect we base our whole legal system with more reliance on what people saw, than what they heard.

Moving on to hearing, like light sound is a oscillating wave of energy emitting out from its origin which is usually a resonance in a material object, energy is pushed into a piece of matter, such as our vocal cords, converted into motion that creates resonant waves of energy in the air, which in turn reaches our eardrums, they vibrate and match this resonance, and again these get converted into data which gets passed to our brain and presented as sound to be interpreted and rationalised against our experience. Audio speakers work pretty much the same way, as do microphones, microphones like our ears have a thin film which is subjected to tiny vibrations in the air known as sound waves, these vibrations in the film, cause changes to a magnetic field as it shakes the receptor that sits in the magnets, this change in the magnetic fields alters the flow of electricity producing a sequence of data that in digital recording is converted into ones and zeros, the binary that is then stored in their sequences as files in our MP3 players which can be replayed or used to be amplified through our TV sets internal speakers. Speakers are larger cones of film, who magnets are moved by electrical energy to turn this data back into motion, when attached to the paper or film of speakers, causes vibrations that travel through the air and are in turn caught by our ears when we are listening to our gaming buddy from in-game chat. In fact, in the modern world we live in, we strive towards fully immersive virtual reality for all our needs, entertainment being the forerunner, but in time we will be completely at home with immersive reality worlds for most aspects of our lives. Business meetings will be done by immersive virtual boardrooms, this will be led by cost reduction, no more will people feel the need to Jet off to Hong Kong or even from home to work for an exchange of views that are "face to face", our families will be projected into our homes and interact with us no matter where they are in the world, with enough data, who knows they may not even need to be living do this, maybe we will subscribe to virtual wives, husbands and children existing in a virtual home that is a projection of an artificial home made up of a corporately "sold" idea of harmonic existence.

Our more immediate future will probably be based around a VR headset such as the emerging Oculus rift, as time passes, probably less cumbersome and more compact and less ridiculous looking, augmented reality contact lenses and ear implants will become the norm for a continuous connection to a virtual world.

Holographic rooms such as we see on fantasy programs like Star-Trek, will be, without doubt a reality. At first, they will use a combination of augmented reality, projected backdrops and integration with body mounted enhancements such as earpieces and motion resistance suits. But as time passes, soft lasers could track and fire 3D imagery direct into our eyes, or maybe development of artificial imagery devices for blind people that convert a camera image into neural data attached direct to the brain could circum-pass the camera and have generated imagery pushed direct to the minds interpreter. All things that can deceive what we conceive as subjective reality can be tricked into believing that our environment is what we see, hear, smell, taste, sense. Nothing is beyond the realms of a technological illusion in the very near future.

So, what is reality? Reality is not a shared experience as you are inclined to believe. It is deeply personal. No two people experience the same reality, even as a shared event in our material universe any two individuals will take from it a slightly differing experience. Even if it is initially a view of an event from two slightly different angles, the previous experience of one of those individuals may produce a completely different understanding of the events that unfolded. To use an extreme example a primitive man seeing a helicopter flying over his isolated village will see a strange magical beast, this is purely due to his lack of understanding of the machine we have come to accept as a natural phenomenon which would probably not even be recounted to our friends unless it did something out of the ordinary, to the primitive man, its legend will be retold as wondrous a mystery as if we had seen what we call a UFO. Experience helps to define our reality, and we all have different subjective realities.

The Facets of Our Lives.

When thinking about the subjective self I realise that we comprise of many people. I cannot imagine that anyone could claim to portrait the same person in all environments and facets of their lives. Sadly, it seems that there is some notion of pride when one claims to be uni-present.

I take an instant dislike when I hear an individual boast "what you see is what you get" or "I speak my mind", believing their claims of brutishness and frankness is somehow a desirable virtue. Rarely do I meet people extoling this claim who then later contribute merit to any endeavour, let alone palatable conversation. Though they may positively believe they hold such a trait, I believe it is an egocentric projection that's validity is concealed in self-delusion. It is simply impossible for anyone to maintain a single aspect of personality all the time. Much like all the rest of us, we cycle and present multiple personalities, personalities most suited to the situation or most suited to the environment and company at the time. We may hold one core self, but that is shielded by personal masks, costumes and pageantry. If we take two very simple examples. Do we behave with the same regard to absolute strangers in the street, as we do our close family, or our children? No, of course we don't, and it would be a terrible state of affairs if we did. So, this claim which a few people boastfully express, instils in me and instant dislike for the person, and to be honest they are being flippant with their respect towards you or I. Showing a complete disregard for your relationship. They quite early in the relationship are saying that they care not if you should like them or not. This flippancy is the catalyst for the "not".

This seems to be a feeble attempt to endorse themselves as honest and frank, and is intended to present them as "down to earth" or a bold claim that their words are to be considered concordant with their mind, yet this brashness then needs to be enforced regardless of any change in situation.

It is a pre-able and a dismissive excuse to behave rudely, if they feel they can. It is a lie. So, why would I begin with a rant about personality? Because todays subject is about personality, how we believe we have one. My claim is that we do not, we have many. We present ourselves in different situations and to different groups of relationships with an entirely different persona, not exactly ground-breaking, but it is important to make consideration upon this to understand our personal ego. Understanding the self forms the larger body of the Luciferian path. Any person of a socially acceptable mind-set, will switch personality modes to be compliant with the social environment. They will regulate their projection of unfiltered thoughts to that which are considered acceptable in that environment. I would suggest that anyone who is not capable of this, will probably struggle socially and more importantly struggle vocationally, ending up in menial, manual labour jobs. You must embrace your aspects of self. The demons and the angels that present and eternal turmoil or harmony within you. As god of your personally occupied area of the universe you should consider yourself like a fine cocktail of exotic flavours and spices. Indulge yourself in the ones that you favour, but remember that not all spices are to everyone's taste. To take advantage of every individual you meet, you should offer them the drink that they enjoy. When you offer a guest tea, for example, you politely ask do you like that with milk. Sugar?

The same applies to how they take you. You should know the correct amount of milk, and sugar to the taste provided to your guest.

Ingratiate your guest, ingratiate everybody, and be nice. It is endemic of people who identify themselves with the Left-Hand Path to indulge an aura of their dark side, it bolsters the ego when people have a trepidation around you. But what does that achieve? It achieves caution, fear, mistrust and certainly no loyalty. If you want to succeed using true wisdom, then realise that the truest dark side is not fashion or black clothes and satanic symbols. It is embracing the psychopath with. The psychopath is not evil, or malicious, he is objective. He manipulates his environment. This is the keystone of success.

You will get far more rewards from massaging other people's egos than you will complaining at their incompetence. Smile, tell them how wonderful they are at their work, let them think they are really important to you. Have you never experienced customer service? Your call is very important to us, or have a nice day? You don't believe it in most cases, it's just company patter, but you think they do that to be nice? No for some fools they believe that the person serving them a hamburger is concerned that the rest of their customer's day goes wonderfully.

Be a manipulator, learn the skills, only then will you recognise the true people to hold in your life. I know, your instinct is to reject this notion, you are a nice person. So am I, believe me.

We are taught from an early age that honesty is a virtue, be nice to people and be honest, that we should not "use" people. But that's the first step the manipulators used to get you to be manipulated. From that moment, you were the hunted. And I'm not suggesting you be an arsehole to everyone you meet. I'm suggesting that you only show your true loving self to those that eventually deserve it.

Be nice, in fact, be nicer than you have ever been, be supportive, be positive, and help people when they need it. But don't be a sucker. If you tell people that you work with how excellent their contribution was to your project, they will "like" you. They cannot help it. Flatter them, don't go overboard and appear like a stalker. Notice hair changes, compliment people on looks, shoes, particularly things they have taken pride in, like art or poetry. This will create an inability to criticise you. To the extent that they will feel compelled to return the favour. Give to receive, my nephew was working at a bar, he averaged around £4 tips a day. I suggested to him that whenever he had time, it was a busy bar that while serving a customer, make an extra journey to their table. That he should take some nonchalant gift, sauces, extra napkins, straws for children. Say to them, "If you want anything else just wave me across and I'll come and help you". But, to do it as a separate journey. When handing the gifts over, he should say "I, thought you could use these" emphasising the "I" because what that does is separates the individual, from the business. They have looked at the price-list, they know what they are getting as part of the package. But know "I" (he) has gone over providing additional, complimentary gifts to the agreed list price. Subconsciously the people receiving have been programmed to return gifts for gifts, upon leaving the business establishment. They pay the amount agreed, but now feel obliged, and pleased to return the favours to the individual who went above the service menu.

If they ask for anything out of the ordinary, explain "well, 'I' am not supposed to but, of course, for you". That day he brought home £26 in tips. In this example, he separated the purchase deliverables from his personally added deliverables, even though they were included in the service. By making people believe that that the personal touch was because he was particularly nice, the people felt they needed to reward him personally. The same resides in any work, flatter your boss, tell them they are the best boss you ever had. Assuming they have not read this book, they will see you as an underling prodigy, you will be rewarded with the training and the promotions. You will notice in work that when you are dealing with customers, you are subconsciously compelled to speak for the company with the term "We". Yet those in higher regard in the company will always make personal pledges "I". They have taken personal responsibility for the issue resolution; the customer feels like they are getting a personal service from a manager. And all the "we's" are impersonal masses, not worthy of recognition.

Become an "I".

It is good practice to maintain this façade wherever possible, practicing it makes for a deeper, more layered and complex character set that we can use to our advantage. You must embrace your personalities, they are not a disorder. They are your internal aspects, nor is this a dishonest trait, it simply is a matter of reserving the heavy artillery, and using it sparingly, only when we have escalated dialogue to where graciousness has failed. Aspects I have written of in my previous works, are my alternative term for what many will call "Demons" or "Angels". They are independent personality traits which constantly battle for supremacy of our consciousness.

Aspects can be considered flavours of conscious, sentient but sharing our instance of consciousness. They are metaphysical in structure, they like the gnostic God of the universe are both within and without us. We are not separate from them, but they exist separate from us. If you need the physics of this explained in layman's terms. I can put it quite simply. Imagine the universe as a sealed unit, like a tank of water. Water, is fluid, it is the spirit of life, it is our consciousness. If the material aspect of we, is more solid, our bodies are a container for the spirit. We can imagine this like a bottle, dropped into the tank. You can put lots of bottles into the tank, these all represent different people and each bottle has no lid, they fill with the water of the tank, absorbing their shared environment. In nice clean water, we are all the same. But let's put a bottle in that contains red dye, its red dye, leaks out, it is concentrated in that one bottle, but before long the water turns pink, and most bottles have an equal amount of red dye. Consider this an aspect, a demon or an angel. Now let us suggest that instead of one dye, there are lots of coloured dyes. But these dyes wont blend together, a bottle will contain ¼ red, ¼ blue, ¼ green and ¼ yellow. And the yellow remains an entity unto itself. It is the aspect of yellow. Each bottle happily shares a balance of colours as does the tank universe.

Our individual personalities mean we are not identical so while we still contain 100% liquid, we may be 27% yellow,

13% red, 40% green and 20% blue. The universe as a contained system will always find balance, yet as individuals we can indulge one aspect of our personality more. Let us say that yellow represents Jealousy. By feeling jealous we encourage more yellow dye into our body, we feed it and it grows, make our clear glass bottle emit only yellow jealousy, pushing out other aspects of ourselves.

We call the yellow from elsewhere in the universe and become the "embodiment" of jealousy. The natural dichotomic antonym to jealousy is contentment. If we say for our example that contentment is blue, then this will be the first colour to be evicted from our bottle, to be replaced by yellow. It's as simple as that. But there is one other sinister angle to this simplistic parallel. The aspects (colours) are sentient in themselves. This is what we need to understand to practice demonolatry, and understand the purpose of demonology.

The yellow dye, despite being dispersed amongst separate bottles, and floating around in a tank, uncaptured in an individual, is a true spirit of nature. It may present itself as 20% of one person, and 5% of another person. But the 100% of jealousy is true to itself, it is not restricted by physical locations and the three-dimensional space of our physical universe, it is pure spirit. And the practice of demonolatry is knowing how to communicate directly with this spirit. Because when you do, you are not communicating with the 5% of you that it manifests in. you are communicating with it as a whole, you are communicating with the entire universes jealousy. And you can ask it to work in others.

If you have an interest in demonolatry you must start here. Understanding how to master the aspects in your own mind. Once you understand them, and can manipulate or influence them in your own bottle, you can then look to influence the whole tank. This simple principle will allow you mastery over the aspects in other peoples and ultimately with the entity itself in in independent form.

Each day we create many artificial worlds, each one wears the representation you wish to create with your specific demographic. You actively manage the balance of these aspects which ultimately produces who you are to the individuals you meet during your day. Referring to our dishes analogy, we sweeten our taste and milk it according to the desires of the drinker. When we talk in the occult circles about demon's people often take a great leap from what we consider our everyday demons, like "alcoholism" which is usually linked to some driving aspect of abolishment from reality, or a "vice", or an emotion that represents itself as "anger" issues into some huge leap to a horned monster that is summoned from the pits of hell. But, they are one in the same, they too have their aspects or method of interacting with you. For some reason, Hollywood and prophets of doom will have you divide aspects by some great chasm. One being just a personal hang-up and the other being the stuff of fairytale or worse a malevolent force that you should shy away from, even those proclaiming to be masters of demonolatry, wizards, witches will warn you to avoid any contact with these entities. This is their lack of understanding, being inverted into some mystical knowledge they pretend to have, but hide to protect you. You don't need protecting, these aspects you have dealt with all your life. Now is the time to indulge them as a master. No, if you have an interest, let's explore it. Let's push those demons out and summon them from within, master them. So, demons 101 (from this point on called aspects as they are neither negative nor positive, they are what you use them to be. The only difference is that most people by their own nature, not "super-nature" harmonise the aspects every day. Each internal aspect is held at bay in our very own psyche, we control it, and we exercise it at our will. The portion of their entirety that shares our physicality and our consciousness, we are masters of. These creatures that live within our spiritual mind, and exists outside our containing physicality, Gnosticism presents these as the angels and demons that rebelled against god for his command that they should be subservient to man. But this is only applicable to those we command in our single consciousness; the other portion is free until we become one with the greater collective consciousness "God" if you like. God, the ultimate aspect, our crossover consciousness. Like the aspects, we are God, in that we are a part of the dishes, the whole that makes up the one. Defining the aspects. Some are considered righteous, some considered evil, "Love" for example is one of the more powerful of these entities, he is a close relation of desire, and hate. Yet, someone you love can usually hurt you a lot more than someone you hate.

Occult – That Which is Unseen.

This lesson is on the word occult. When one enters into the studies of the occult it has been in my experience that it is essential to think greatly about significant words. These words that occur commonly in discussions are often read and dismissed with their immediate definition absorbed into the context of the discourse. Wisdom is one of these words, as a Luciferian my driving force is not that of knowledge, but that of wisdom. Dominion over the wise path requires knowledge as its guide to the destination of house of the wise. But the knowledge can be lost and forgotten, but the destination of wisdom is eternal once received.

What is strange that when I "google" this word I get a new definition, contrary to that in which I was brought up to understand.

> Noun: mystical, supernatural, or magical powers, practices, or phenomena.

> "a secret society to study alchemy and the occult".

> synonyms: the supernatural, the paranormal, supernaturalism, magic, black magic, witchcraft, sorcery, necromancy, wizardry, the black arts, Kabbalah, cabbalism, occultism, diabolism, devil worship, devilry, voodoo, hoodoo, white magic, witchery, witching, orenda, mysticism.

It seems nowadays the guides to educational sources have corrupted the nature of this word which in time will be forever associated with "hocus pocus". This corruption is commonplace. Knowledge; true knowledge is globally conspired to be hidden from the common man. I, and you I presume are the common man.I rebel against such things being kept from me, and I try, in my humble way to explain the truths and to ensure that the wicked do not corrupt the good name of Lucifer. Seekers of truth, dismiss those that teach the Bible the organized church, but do not dismiss the Bible. One day though you may resent it now because of what the preachers have made this book represent. I am hopeful that you will have become enlightened enough to understand that which was written in the divine pages of the book.

Occult, some of you are aware has the real meaning of "what is unseen, hidden" from its Latin etymological roots and indeed the Bible is a sourcebook of the occult by very definition. Within those pages are the studies of men, advanced beyond their time in terms of philosophy, astronomy, and astrology. Secret knowledge that had to be written in abstract nonsensical metaphors, so that that it could be passed to those who have knowledge of decoding those metaphors to predict the great cosmic calendar and events that are cyclic as all things truly are. What is unseen, is not a definition of what is out of sight, out of sight may simply be something clearly visible to most, but obscured to the blind or those that choose to close their eyes. As a matter of perspective, light or illumination is not merely restricted to the optical range of wavelength, illumination can be transmitted by touch, or sound by vibration or excitement of a receptive device to a transmitting device.

What cannot be seen, is one's self. Exploration of the occult is the exploration of one's self. The inner sense is the destination of those seeking wisdom. It is only by truly being able to access the deeply hidden root persona of IAM that one connects with the universal spirit shared by all life. When we gain mastery over communing with IAM, we can influence IAM the root self within others. This is true prayer, commune with God and the greater spiritual universe.

The Ancient cult of the Ox

The cult of the ox, BAAL, BAËL, the Bull

The ages we attribute to religion are etched into the collective psyche of man. It is almost as though a supreme force is dictating our narrative of the divine provenance and it holds no regard of our collective efforts and schemes to force spiritual beliefs and philosophies in any given direction. The eons of the astrological cycle still cause their apocalypses on man with the certainty and regularity of a new sunrise. History seems to dictate that what is now will be criticized by our descendants as we criticize those before us. All that light must become dark and all truth will become lies. There is no facts, this principle I maintain from my first journey into philosophy.

You will find as you progress in your learning that the current Piscean dogma that has hold over the world in its manifestations as Christianity, Judaism, Islam will like all its previous aeons become tainted with time, but it will not just fade away and be forgotten as misconception, no it will be vilified and become hated by those that see themselves as progressive; this is nothing new, The calf God is vilified in the bible, as was the arian goat god before him. It takes no great leap of the mind to see where the symbology of the horned gods which are now used to depict devils and wayward beleifs were inherrited from ages past. This vilification of the previous aeons will continuew, and our wonderful age of Aquarious, the Aeon of Lucifer will once again fall fowl to the next aeonetic apocolypse.

In just over two millenia that which is the birth of the child of enlightenment will be looked back upon, as we look back upon Jesus today, with doubt, scepticism, and resentment to the destruction it has caused, but from this side of the dawn, we see only hope, blessings of hindsight arives upon the shoulders of those who bore its darkest hours. And many will doubt the great events tht are our today. Imagine something like the internet described in those times, a single connected world, where all information could be read, the knowledge of the world. It almost describes the Library of Babylon doesn't it. And who knows what dark ages of destruction will come between now and then, a loss of technology, energy, electricty, wars and famine could leave our technological age merely a whim of fantasy and fairytale, with many doubting it ever couldve happened at all.

Throughout all these time, there has been but one God, what changes is "the Lord" which is the primary path to that god. He takes to form of a supernatural being, often a God made flesh. Most would describe him as a prophet of some sort, a Christ or simply the holiest of men. Their teachings become so large that it cannot be accepted that they are mere mortals and so the attributes as being "a God who walks amongst men" in bestowed upon them along with Godlike abilities. But they are simply make, half-truth, half legend and wrapped in an ancient hermetic truth which allows it to resonate with men. For what are men if we cannot become gods. To divide ourselves from god is to make ourselves slaves and slaves to an all-powerful god will eternally be slaves, yet if one man can become Herculean in strength and stand equal with gods, half-man, half all, then we have hope. These ancient teachings although cyclic and worshiping the same God via different paths, must reflect that God not as an individual but as his current celestial manifestation. Those that study the Occult are members of the demonized oculus and enlightenment of the truth behind religion are frowned up and rejected by those that seek power to manipulate using the control system built into faith. These people are the corrupted ones. Do not get me wrong and despise those worshippers of the Piscean God, they for their most part are good people, content in their ignorance. It was Gods will that man should remain ignorant; Lucifer brought enlightenment to those who choose to see the bigger picture. Again, this is commonly thought of as a blessing, but duality will dictate that "ignorance is bliss" and so knowledge is a curse equal to a blessing.

If life is as cyclic as the rest of the universe, then it is probably the case that those seeking enlightenment are further down the cosmic road than the ones whose current incarnation does not. Help your fellow man by empathy to a time when you were less wise. Guide them but do not despise them, hatred a reflective manifestation of their hatred towards you. Reject this notion, we are the parents, they are children.

Occult, the worship of one's self. Not the abstract self, not ego, not individuality, but the innermost self, that shared by all mankind. In Gnostic Luciferianism, God exists as an amalgamation of all consciousness, it is the collective knowledge and wisdom shared with all universe and the universe is God's body. All things in the universe are a component part of God and as hands of God, we work together, as alone we are as unproductive as a rock. It is by the flow and cooperation of the cosmos around us that we can create and lay our table as we desire.

The word Occult derived in the 15th century from the Latin word Oelare > Occuler – you can see the similarity to our modern-day word unclear then later from the evolved into french word "Occulte".Ob=Over, Celare=To hide.

And then other related words would be ob-solete, Ob being to hide, Sol the sun. Obsolete is to hide the sun or the light. We now take this word as being out of date, as are the Taurean and Arian Ages.

Ob is a Hebrew word and as all Hebrew words a single word can have many meanings but are all related. Ob is a skin that us used to carry water. It is also a Necromancer. The skin clearly is a dead animal hide and most likely ram or bovine, Ob-vine. Vine, vitality or lineage. So, pertaining in all ways to "the path of the Dead Bull". If you wish to learn the occult ways, then be prepared to learn the forgotten wisdom of the obsolete Gods.

Deuteronomy 18-

Deuteronomy means Mosaic (teachings of Moses, Moslaw – (modern day Muslim)) Law, Deuteronomy is the fifth book of Pentateuch (Pentateuch: is the first five books of the Old Testament (five-teachings)) one for each of the points of the pentagram, each contain 72 degrees of enlightenment, complimentary to the 360 degrees of the full cycle.

> 1 The priests the Levites, and all the tribe of Levi, shall have no part nor inheritance with Israel: they shall eat the offerings of the Lord made by fire, and his inheritance. 2 Therefore shall they have no inheritance among their

> brethren: the Lord is their inheritance, as he hath said unto them. 3 And this shall be the priest's due from the people, from them that offer a sacrifice, whether it be ox or sheep; and they shall give unto the priest the shoulder, and the two cheeks, and the maw.

here you can see specific mention of the ram and the ox, Taurus and Aries, Moses and his descents the tribe of Moses are one of the seven tribes of Israel known as the tribe of Levi. Levi was the son of Jacob and were a nomadic tribe, so that would indicate a nomadic star as their iconic representation the wondering stars were planets as all other stars are fixed relative to each other from the earth centric point of view. Since the sacrificial offering is to give up, Aries and Taurus, you are now to worship the fish. The fisher of men, Pisces will me the constellation that the sun god was currently in manifestation in. The shoulder, two cheeks and maw state specifically the area in which the Sun and associated wandering planet was in at that time.

> 4 The first fruit also of thy corn, of thy wine, and of thine oil, and the first of the fleece of thy sheep, shalt thou give him. 5 For the Lord thy God hath chosen him out of all thy tribes, to stand to minister in the name of the Lord, him and his sons for ever. 6 And if a Levite come from any of thy gates out of all Israel, where he sojourned, and come with all the desire of his mind unto the place which the Lord shall choose;

Corn and wine and oil are known as fruits of the earth, "food, drink and fuel". Corn is associated with the Egyptian god Isis as it is a symbol of rebirth and renewal all these things shall be rewarded to you at this time. "minister in the name of the Lord" small star (mini-star) in the name of the lord is a description of the alignment of the sun, the planet (minister) and the constellation these three elements (letters) make the word (name) of the lord.

> 7 Then he shall minister in the name of the Lord his God, as all his brethren the Levites do, which stand there before the Lord. 8 They shall have like portions to eat, beside that which cometh of the sale of his patrimony. 9 When thou art come into the land which the Lord thy God giveth thee, thou shalt not learn to do after the abominations of those nations.

Once the astronomy is understood as you see it in the sky it will be a time of good provision for the earth Patrimony means literally fathers-money or property inherited from one's father or male ancestor. So, this means to renew yourself by relinquishing the old ways and embracing the new astrological age.

> 10 There shall not be found among you any one that maketh his son or his daughter to pass through the fire, or that useth divination, or an observer of times, or an enchanter, or a witch, 11 Or a charmer, or a consulter with familiar spirits, or a wizard, or a necromancer. 12 For all that do these things are an abomination unto the Lord:

and because of these abominations the Lord thy God doth drive them out from before thee.

13 Thou shalt be perfect with the Lord thy God.

14 For these nations, which thou shalt possess, hearkened unto observers of times, and unto diviners: but as for thee, the Lord thy God hath not suffered thee so to do.

15 ¶The Lord thy God will raise up unto thee a Prophet from the midst of thee, of thy brethren, like unto me; unto him ye shall hearken;

16 According to all that thou desirest of the Lord thy God in Horeb in the day of the assembly, saying, Let me not hear again the voice of the Lord my God, neither let me see this great fire any more, that I die not.

17 And the Lord said unto me, they have well-spoken that which they have spoken.

18 I will raise them up a Prophet from among their brethren, like unto thee, and will put my words in his mouth; and he shall speak unto them all that I shall command him.

19 And it shall come to pass, that whosoever will not hearken unto my words which he shall speak in my name, I will require it of him.

20 But the prophet, which shall presume to speak a word in my name, which I have not

commanded him to speak, or that shall speak in the name of other gods, even that prophet shall die.

21 And if thou say in thine heart, how shall we know the word which the Lord hath not spoken?

22 When a prophet speaketh in the name of the Lord, if the thing follow not, nor come to pass, that is the thing which the Lord hath not spoken, but the prophet hath spoken it presumptuously: thou shalt not be afraid of him.

The Abyss.

The eternal tunnel is a shared memory of every sentient lifeform in the universe. Since your birth, you have had this often-forgotten fear of the eternal tunnel. It does not always present itself in your primary consciousness, instead it lurks at the back of your mind and appears in moments of anxiety, stress, fear, dread or dreams. It can be induced by drugs or by people who have mortal fear thrown upon them for one reason or another, where they perceive a real state of an impending end of life.

You haven't talked about the tunnel to others as you dismiss it as simply your own, personal imagination, but it is not. It is a shared experience from a millennium before your current incarnation. It is the demon pit from which you have emerged after spending a true eternity existing within it, and your biggest fear when facing death is that you will return to it.

Forever falling into an inescapable doom and dread of eternal solitude, a solitude that is incomparable to human loneliness, a solitude which is not simply presenting yourself alone and absent from friends, a solitude that can only be compared to being the only thing in the universe, the only thing in all universes.

Nobody speaks of the tunnel, and you are surprised by these words, as you believed it was only you who remembers and fears it, deep down you know it is not a dream, you know it is not imagination, it is a pre-birth memory.

You have no recollection of ever reaching the bottom of the tunnel, but the fear of the eternal doom which lies beneath is terrifying. It is all you believe the worst of death to be. None existence and an eternity of nothing, not even an imagination to distract you from the reality, just pure vivid experience of the tunnel, forever.

Despite your toying with the idea that Hell might be a fun place, you know this place is not fun, you know this place is nothing at all, this is true damnation, no punishment, no fires, no anything. Just your consciousness and eternal falling deeper into that which is below.This is the collective experience of us, all life existed once in its collective form, before the creation of the universe.

We as a shared singularity of all consciousness experienced this as a single individual, which is why it is a shared secret of us all, a distant, forgotten or vague memory of all life, not just all people, all things capable of thought share this memory.

Some people experience the Tunnel in NDEs (Near Death Experiences), one website appropriates this tunnel to the trauma of childbirth, and which is I suppose valid in that it's a post-cognitive memory, it may seem more viable to our material universe, particularly those who have not yet been able to transverse the limitations of the material bound mind. The MBM (material bound mind) is a person who wholly rejects matters of spirituality and can only conceive the world as it is presented to him in its physical law-abiding presentation, time, dimensions, cause and effect. The material bound mind is a popular culture in modern man which has grown as a result of the rejection of spiritual concepts.

Spiritual concepts in this day and age are seemingly bound to corrupt religious orders, which have over the course of history, proven themselves not to be trustworthy in its care for man's extra-material affairs. They have behaved inappropriately with the spiritual nature of both the soul and the organization of humanity, and all have played their part.

Religious organisations have preyed on the weakness and beliefs of mankind to a point of frenzy, murder and diabolicalness, creating absolute fear at worst or indifference at best to the greater body of consciousness that we are universally a part of.

It has come to the point where people are so disenfranchised with their very own spiritual self at the hands of the churches, mosques and synagogues and religious zealots, who either go around telling anyone who "they" them believe to be different that "they're" us are going to hell, or even worse killing or hurting someone for simply believing in a different path to a "peaceful" life.

The two scourges on humanity are both worthy of despise, and most likely to go to any proverbial Hell than any of the rest of us (yes that's you Mr holier than though bible belt supremacist). These people rather than save souls as their prophets instructed them to, use their religion as a form of artificial-superiority and cause sensible people to identity as atheists, rather than get embroiled in an endless row over which sky fairy is the real one. As frustrating as this is to me, it is understandable.

And what of the material bound mind who requires quantifiable substance to believe something exists?

I simply say this, measure your love for someone, and then hold the love in front of them on a platter for them to see, and if you cannot, then by your law, love does not exist.

The Earth's Second Sun.

As I try to rationalise pre-Common-Era concepts of divinity and their respective view of the universe. I, like anyone else will find reoccurring common themes which present themselves across nations, creeds and mythos. These common elements that you try to de-mystify are so embedded within the mysticisms and writings that I find them almost impossible to ignore or underestimate their significance those cultures. Though, abundant with different possible specific definitions, they all form a similar underlying theme; that you are left to conclude that they have a truth that is tantalisingly obvious, yet unspecific in ways which we understand with todays evolved use of expanded language. To put it simply, I return to the idea of a common root language or having words that appropriated their definition while spoken in context. These words applied to many items that had at the time not yet evolved a compartmentalised or specific characteristic which was explicit to itself.

As these concept words transverse continents and time periods, they developed analogies localised to that time and place. This resulted in a mishmash of tales, folklore, legend and creed we try to interpret today as separate concepts, but in reality, share their origins.

The literal interpretations of these localised and embellished stories form the diversity of pre-literal idioms we try to interpret today.

This diversity forms the endless discussions and scholarly argument of esoteric interpretation we encounter today, of which I'm equally guilty. This is the breeding ground which bears the child of the eternal conflict where man's stupidity leads him to argue that "my god is the one true god, and all others are pretenders to the throne". The worst possible outcome is that they throw out all their moral stances to the point of bloodshed and hatred. Ironically, if their creed has any themes of love and respect for their fellow men, they disregard that concept with vigour as they rush to declare holy wars and exterminate or at very least vilify all their subjective adversary figures. Demonising them in a very literal sense of the word satanic.

Assuming their singular "God" or "Heaven" and "eternal damnation" rhetoric to be true, then this vile face of religion is more responsible for condemning the souls of none believers than any mistaken belief in the "wrong god". Since their condemnation and aggression towards anyone who is "he who is not like us" resultantly drives rational people to avoid religion all together, dismiss spirituality as wholly nonsense and to embrace only the material nature of their existence. The result being that since material or physical science is far less ambiguous in its explicit definition it becomes, for the most part far-less troublesome.

Of course, some atheists are equally as fundamentally irrational as the orthodox religious zealots in their conviction and desire to overthrow anyone who chooses to think differently; As much like the 'bible bashing' fanatic who insists upon condemning your mortal soul based on his subjective view of reality, the atheist zealots also shove their subjective beliefs down your throat and condemn anyone who doesn't share their views.

Fortunately, in both camps there exist the rational people who are happy just to 'live and let live'. Yet despite this rational view of the whole debacle I sadly find myself a zealot, insistent on writing his beliefs like some modern-day prophet, pretending he has all the answers.

In my defence, I am open to be enlightened, I don't believe I have it 'all worked out'. My role in this as alluded to in the opening chapter is to share with you that which I discover and believe may be true. If you don't find it fits with your belief, then neither you or I are wrong, we simply exist in a different subjective universe for the moment and are as divinely correct as anyone else. My drive is to learn from you, debate and maybe between us we will one day become Godlike in our wisdom, less fanatically convinced our viewpoint is correct and the world, indeed the universe will be a better more sympathetic and respectful place towards other sovereign souls.

Now with that pre-amble declaimer of my approach to this theory I jump into the shock jock style headline of this paper 'The Earths Second Sun'.

Now you may assume that I'm going to explain some metaphysical representation of this emotive headline, but I am not. I am going to present to you some of the many concepts, texts and evidence that the earth did indeed at one point have in the heavens an astrological body that could be compared to a binary system, a second sun.

First, I will present the three hypothesis that would make this true, then I will analyse each of them using the information that either correlates or impugns the case.

1. Our solar system had an internal illuminated body that is no longer in the solar system.
2. Our solar system has a planetary body that once was brightly illuminated as a nearby star or was a star and is now extinguished or less comparable to a nearby star.
3. An extra-solar (supernova) was close enough or large enough to be perceived as a second sun.

Now that the scope of the investigation has been laid out I will begin with some of the stories and fables that are shared throughout the world which could be interpreted as being historical legend of the earth's second sun.

Some of this may contradict my previously written interpretations in books and papers, but as I suggested in my preamble, I am of no illusion that anything I have ever said is fact, "in fact"- *he says contradicting himself,* I regularly point out that there is no such thing as facts, just subjective and collective opinions, formed by best guesses and evidence presented at the time. I continue to learn and re-evaluate that which I held true on a daily basis, if we all did this instead of insisting our beliefs are absolute, then maybe we could get that peaceful earth we all dream of.

I am not a scientist, I am not an expert in any fields, I am purely someone who indulges in objective and holistic views of subjects be and posits conclusions; which I consider have merit. I am happy to learn I was wrong, because accepting we were wrong brings about true knowledge, whereas insisting we are correct regardless of evidence, well that is for the fools, and sadly this is a concept that is holding back the evolution of mankind, not just by religious zealots, but by scientists, who are too frightened to put their reputation on the line or to reject the party line for fear of being ostracised by their scientific community.

I implore experts and thinkers to throw out these rulebooks, say all that you think possible, lets debate the most outlandish ideas, to the point where we can say with absolute certainty, "that cannot be because…".

First Posit. Our solar system had an internal illuminated body that is no longer in the solar system.

I will be the first to admit that in my opinion this would be the least likely of the three situations. Although many people and cultures have laid out evidence that support a few different incarnations of our current solar system.

Mankind as Homo sapiens which we interpret to mean modern humans rather than our more animalistic predecessors have roamed the earth for 200,000 years I am informed by those that study our evolution. We quickly dismiss these men as being simple, almost animals themselves, but it really is a description of modern man, with the brain power equal to what we have now, just lacking the complexities of its use. If we think to the simplistic life of the times of Jesus, basic tools, pottery, shelter, buildings, writing, sea travel, international relationships. Most of those have existed for at least four to eight thousand years before that, seems like a long time, but if you think of one-hundred years as three generations, you to your grandparents, each hundred years is equivalent to that contemporary exchange of life spans and two-thousand years is just twenty iterations of those relationships. So, if you consider the idea of yourself as a child speaking to your grandparent, and them speaking to theirs, that's only twenty times backwards for that to happen to get to the times of Jesus, sixty to get back to the times when we have no accurate written history. Between eight thousand years ago and two-hundred-thousand years ago, is an extremely long time where not much changed in man's development it seems. But we were capable. And we spoke, we travelled the earth and we exchanged stories. We shared an earth and if that earth had two bright suns, one which is no longer there, it would be a huge story passed down by word of mouth, since we did not write. Imagine homo-sapiens lifespan as your own, in your infancy you did not write your experience, but you still to this day, in company, lament times of things you saw and witnessed, you may even have had some historic grandparent to which you have told stories to your children who in turn will say how their great grandfather may fought in the boar war. As you develop and age, you could well write down your great grandfather's story, but you certainly wouldn't begin such as an infant.

We believe that the solar system was formed from a cosmic chaos of matter and bodies colliding, exploding, fusing and separating. Put simply it is inconceivable that all the planets formed at the same time, indeed evidence such as the asteroid belt, and our current understanding of planet formation would suggest that planets are still being formed today. The assumption is that gravitational waves emanating from the most gravitas celestial body, in our case the Sun, creates the field which causes resting places for these orbiting collections of debris, which ultimately fuses to form a new planet. They start out somewhat like the rings of Saturn, but obviously on a much larger and dispersed scale, and eventually gather together attracting each component to another. Personally,

I'm not that comfortable with this, but these are the summations of men greater than I.

This presents an undeniable conclusion that the universe and more specifically localised to us, our solar system is subject to immense change in its dynamic relationship to its components. Planets certainly come from somewhere. Theories proposed, such as our Earth's moon (Luna) did not always belong to the earth and that somehow, we "caught" it as it was floating by are also posited and similarly we can also throw this into a mix of possibilities with regards to how the plants arrived in our solar system, but it doesn't help to suggest how they were formed.

In-fact there's a few ideas behind this moon capture theory, one of which is coined "Giant impact theory" which was first proposed in the 1970s – this theory poses that the moon was formed after the earth collided with an unknown other cosmological body possibly the size of another planet, mars was given as an example.

"It is known that giant collisions are a common aspect of planet formation," said Erik Asphaug of the University of California-Santa Cruz. In 2001 a computer simulation supported the mathematics behind this theory and that it would've possibly happened if this theory is correct, just after the earth's formation four-and-a-half billion years ago.

What this presents to support our theory is that huge astrological bodies in the past freely roamed around our solar system, their frequency and if indeed when they happened can only be speculation. Any evidence that exists to prove conclusively that this is what happened, has so long since disappeared that we can present no historical evidence today that it ever happened.

Because four-and-a-half billion years kind of finds an equilibrium, 1 billion years of the passage of time makes it incredibly difficult to say, "this is what happened" for sure.

We also can see in our skies currently existing [3]*binary star systems*, solar systems which indeed have two stars. How they interact and form is still speculation, does one Sun in these solar systems eventually become dominant, throwing the other one out or do they collide and ultimately fuse to form one larger star? As yet, we don't know?

Between Mars and Jupiter, sitting between a hundred and ten and two hundred and five million miles from the earth there exists a ring of debris we know more commonly as "the" asteroid belt. It being our solar systems primary asteroid belt, we call the moon "the" and the sun "the", not because they are the only ones, but because they are the most significant ones pertaining to our view of the universe.

The first thing I bring to your attention after making that disclaimer is that according to Wikipedia, the origin of Human language is "in dispute", but that simple first paragraph entry, shows how we can trust certain things to Wikipedia, there is therefore no dispute, that the origins of language are not in dispute. And then it goes on to say:-

---

[3] A binary star is a star system consisting of two stars orbiting around their common barycentre. Systems of two, three, four, or even more stars are called multiple star systems – Wikipedia

"This shortage of empirical evidence has led many scholars to regard the entire topic as unsuitable for serious study. In 1866, the linguistic society of Paris banned any existing or future debates on the subject, a prohibition which remained influential across much of the western world until late in the twentieth century. Today, there are numerous hypotheses about how, why, when, and where language might have emerged. Despite this, there is scarcely more agreement today than a hundred years ago, when Charles Darwin's theory of evolution by natural selection provoked a rash of armchair speculation on the topic. Since the early 1990s, however, a number of linguists, archaeologists, psychologists, anthropologists, and others have attempted to address with new methods what some consider "the hardest problem in science."

- Wikipedia on the origin of language.

Of course, I have my own ideas regarding the evolution of word phonetics and meaning, without a great deal of discussion on languages geographical expansion and the anthropological route it took. More just on the word framing and structure itself.

In 1861, historical linguist Max Müller published a list of speculative theories concerning the origins of spoken language.

Bow-wow. the bow-wow or cuckoo theory, which Müller attributed to the German philosopher Johann Gottfried herder, saw early words as imitations of the cries of beasts and birds.

Pooh-pooh. the pooh-pooh theory saw the first words as emotional interjections and exclamations triggered by pain, pleasure, surprise, etc.

Ding-dong. Müller suggested what he called the ding-dong theory, which states that all things have a vibrating natural resonance, echoed somehow by man in his earliest words.

Yo-he-ho. The yo-he-ho theory claims language emerged from collective rhythmic labour, the attempt to synchronize muscular effort resulting in sounds such as heave alternating with sounds such as ho.

Ta-ta. This did not feature in max Müller's list, having been proposed in 1930 by Sir Richard Paget. According to the ta-ta theory, humans made the earliest words by tongue movements that mimicked manual gestures, rendering them audible.

If we simply take the historical view of man and his use (if any) of early language, instead of specifically trying to make a guess, with my little knowledge that would add any contribution to the argument that linguists, archaeologists, psychologists and anthropologists cannot settle upon, and that were not interested in language that relays immediate need, such as primal callings that alert to danger, or are used to form direct contemporary position such as to threaten or frighten or mimic. Then we are only interested in language from when it had developed to an extent that one individual could relay historical or predictive notions to another, when they could reiterate events that where not immediate to the parties concerned, such as relaying events of the day or instruction to do something tomorrow, this would include [4]de ixis which also would've come at a time when man first was able to comprehend subjectivity. Both these topics form most of my approach to the theistic concepts, subjectivity and language. Of course, this period logically presents the similar notion of numeracy. Since man could now conceive the state of I (the eye), the one from whose perception is unique and offered isolation from alternative quantities, numerology, subjectiveness and language formed the new sapiens (wise) man. An ancient wisdom distinguishing the magician from his earliest incarnation as a person who is a little bit more special, than his contemporary [5]"muggle" kin.

Anthropologists and archaeologists generally conclude that such language would coincide with tool advancement, as development of tools would require manipulation in which the tool itself evolved Tool improvement of shape and design would have to be communicated between generations, simple tool use such as using a rock to kill an animal could be

---

[4] In linguistics, deixis refers to words and phrases, such as "me" or "here", that cannot be fully understood without additional contextual information -- in this case, the identity of the speaker ("me") and the speaker's location ("here").

[5] Muggle, taken from J.K. Rowling's, Harry Potter series to describe "normal" folk, people who are not special or magicians or witches. I know its tongue in cheek, but can you think of a better word?

classed as instinctive, but to evolve by sharing how to develop the tool from one person to the next. This would coincide with the early formation of developed rather than appropriated tools and using specific tools for specific purpose according to their form rather than just hitting things. It's not conclusive, but it makes sense.

It is here I throw in my first disagreement with an expert.

Paleoanthropologist [6] Richard G. Klein, claimed that "the Neanderthal brain may have not reached the level of complexity required for modern speech, even if the physical apparatus for speech production was well-developed", seems us Richards all love our language.

This flies in the face of my understanding the standard model of evolution, which I say, simply is "necessity dictates adaption", we don't evolve things we don't use or require. In fact, all I have to this point come to see is that it is quite the reverse. We evolve to lose things we no longer have requirement for, vestigial tail, body hair, appendix and our increased use of what we have, encourages development of that component. The brain, opposing thumbs and I believe an increased requirement to create unique, distinguishable sounds that others could interpret with the same degree of differential meaning all show signs of increased usage. It certainly wouldn't work the other way, in Klein's proposal he seemingly develops physical attributes and components in lieu of potential brain capacity to "catch up".

----

[6] Richard G. Klein (born April 11, 1941) is a Professor of Biology and Anthropology at Stanford University.

The suite of functions that distinguish modern man from his animalistic ancestors is known as [7]Behavioural Modernity. This Klein is a known critic of, but it certainly fits my model, you are free to explore his alternatives, hence my reason to specifically mention him, in the interest that you decide your truth rather than a single subjective opinion. With that I offer Mr Klein my upmost respect, as he presents his belief from his collective evidence and experience instead of just toeing the party line of his peers.

In my take, the evolution of language would not be dependent on the prior evolution of a vocal range, in fact it would not be reliant on vocal method at all, sign language combined with grunts would probably be a precursor, hand gesture and the deixis concept would be enough to convey language outside of a specific vocal class. The primordial instinct to use this is present today when visiting countries where we fail to share language, we quickly resort to a series of imitations and gesturing to help convey our most primal methods of communication, the origins of a universal language.

It is reasonable to conclude that it would be from this point onwards we could claim that some form of language was used to relay information between generations. Any astronomical event witnessed by life on earth or any event that could be communicated to future generations after the event, had occurred for direct contemporary witnesses must have occurred after the development of none immediate language.

---

[7] Behavioural modernity is a suite of behavioural and cognitive traits that distinguishes current Homo sapiens from other anatomically modern humans, hominins, and primates.

The event, in our current proposition is that there was at some point a celestial body whose significance and visibility from the earth would be comparable to the Sun or at least the moon, although I suspect by the archaic legends this object carried a greater influence on the people of the time than the moon, making it the ancient skies at least second, or possibly even most glorious heavenly body, brighter than our current sun.

As I read many-many legendary tales, myths and religious parabolises to seek the knowledge and origins of our modern-day concepts of religion, spirituality and a source of the divine. I am inclined to particularly note their obvious astrological significance, and I have made no doubt in my mind evident of this concept across all my books.

Our skies above are where the first none material Gods were defined, and their words and actions were interpreted into legend by man when he observed the motions and commotions in the heavens.

Our view of the galaxy was akin to the television screen of our ancestors, the animation which formed the celestial evening dance and all the bodies therein defined and foretold apocalypse and the cycles of nature.

Engrained from the earliest formation of what we call man, returning possibly as far back into evolution as when our earliest intelligence was still sea dwelling life or the almost reptilian land fish first crawled from the sea to the trees in search of better survival of our pre-human species, the influence of the skies, sun, moon, tides presented breeding patterns, migration motion and a need to make best advantage of the time of year.

The annual cycle did not have a concept of date to our animal selves, just cycles and patterns that with developing intelligence, became recognisable patterns.

These patterns and the fact that we recognised that the cycles repeated was quite probably the first piece of cognitive function our early brains could realise.

Cycles in the weather and the skies must have had an abstract causation outside the actions of a living individual. Without the greater expansion of experience, we have today cause and effect in our experience was purely the result of intelligent design as all things which move independently in our primitive experience were living creatures. You also should really take on board that familiarity of the year, to us now a simple effect of earth's rotation and orbit of the sun was to the pre-developed mind could only be the result of an exterior mechanism or benefactor which had purpose.

If you combine this simplistic principle, all things that independently move have intelligence, anything that is powerful has some influence over you and has power over you. And so, the wind or sea, which can be kind or cruel to you, must have intelligence and you must pay it reverence or suffer its wrath, and therefore the first Gods were born in man's mind a long time before he was what we call man. In the same way, your pets depend on you, you are principally one stage of a God to your pets.

For early man, the skies were his scrying device and the diviner of man's future. His observations of the sky began with simple weather patterns which could predict essential life supporting principles, even today we are less inclined to take actions based upon even micro-weather patterns on a day to day bases. The forces of the skies are familiar to us today, we understand them better, but for ancient man, the wind was a breath of God, in simplest terms it is conceptually alive and intelligent.

To understand ancient man, we must dismiss science and academia as we have come to understand it. Science, or the accepted knowledge of others as an educational standard, tells us a "what to think" concept that is different to ancient man.

The experience of others was shared only locally, knowledge was gathered only via direct experience, prior to language formation. 98% of everything he knew was as a result of a direct experience within his lifetime. Other things were innate.

Take out your learned knowledge and academia, and relying only on what you have personally witnessed ask yourself why the tide comes in, and goes away, yet the mountains never move? Your answer as a modern man comes from information handed to you from your peers, but without those peers, living in isolation from outside collective knowledge your conclusions would be quite different. The greater percentage of the experience of others which currently form our subjective realities is a modern developed phenomenon. Education in our formative years teaches us certain principles of the way the world works, and by the time we leave school this forms most of our subjective universe and our beliefs.

Rightly or wrongly we rely on this "experience of others" to dictate and form the foundation of everything else we accept as being "reality"

Naturally and predominantly we believe what we are taught, reasonably so we trust that information is without malice and beneficial for us and society. That is true, for society, but not necessarily true for us.

Let us say that in modern man at least 80% to 90% of what he knows is abstract scholarly information and knowledge that is not a result of direct experience, but because of teachings from other sources. One way or another, school, media, books etc. we gather superficial supporting information that helps us establish reasoning to that which we directly experience, to the extent that even our direct experience is built on the foundations of what we have learned, rather than the opposite way of our ancestors whose reality was built on what they experienced and academic knowledge was only accepted when supported by observations due to its lack of availability.

In that sense, most of our reality is not our own subjective experience but that of others, this forms a dilution of that experience and a subjection from the third parties point of view, which we are at risk of.

We are told for example that Pluto is 736miles across. I have absolutely no reason to doubt that and I am not suggesting that people give up science and the knowledge of others in favour of simply believing in the magick of everything, what I am suggesting is that you realise the relevance and perspective of science in relation to the subjective self.

I believe I will never see Pluto in a capacity to measure it, probably neither will you, therefore its size is of no matter, relevance or significance to us, yet still it's an interesting fact if you can remember it. Yet with this information readily available to you to win a point at a pub quiz, how do you know how big Pluto is in reality? Do you really know Pluto even exists? I'm not trying to make a point that Pluto isn't real, I'm making the point of "what is reality" again and in this case the most of it is not what we experience, but what we believe from others. The ancient man without tools such as writing, internet, trusted resources obtained most of his reality from personal experience, therefore they thought entirely differently.

This kind of abstract knowledge is what makes up 80-90% of everything we modern day first-world people know. It may make us look smart at a quiz, but if I was to now tell you that Pluto is in truth one-hundred-and-fifty-thousand miles across, true or false it will never affect your life, this fact is arbitrary to our real lives. You now must go and google to find out how big Pluto is. Your trust in my claims are now with doubt, so you seek collective authority. Similarly, does the earth rotate around the sun, or as we personally observe the sun rises at one side of a flat earth and sets at the other. Science tells us one thing, subjective experience without the benefit of external information tells us another.

And so, to the ancient man, the celestial Gods whom must be intelligent as they move freely around the skies like the birds, can be benevolent or cruel and therefore to seek favour from the Gods, each with their own specific dominion or influence, must be honoured, respected and worshipped as if they look unfavourably upon you, if you do not then you are at risk of their wrath.

Science can be wrong, it often is, because for us wise people, we realise that Science is an evolving collection of observations which are built on previously upheld foundations of knowledge and then current observations using current test methods. When you accept this premise of science (its true premise) rather than that of those "sheeple" that simply believe that material science is god and anything quoted by a "scientist" is therefore proven fact, only then can you objectively look at the nature of our existence.

How often do we find these anti-religion people who quote other people's ideas and share in the credit of the new thought? How often do they say laugh at people who ask the questions of existence rather than explaining arbitrary fact of what, rather than why? They are suffering from subjectivism that is no different from the religious nutters who believe that their "god" is the one true god, both mind-sets are contrary to the evolution of man's greater assentation into establishing us as the greatest intelligence in the universe.

Subjective views opposing each other are blinded by their own origins of perspective. Luciferians balance both equally and use them in our life. Science and Spirituality both offer answers to existence, we do not support one over the other blindly, we support that which we feel more strongly supports our wishes and evidence. And if we find collectively we are straying more towards the religious side of the coin, we need to find the scientific evidence as to why that cannot be true. Likewise, if we find ourselves drifting more towards a material scientific approach, we simply need to remind ourselves to ask the question why rather than how?

What we term Magick is science that is not yet explained and so the pursuit of the powers than make magick is man's inertia towards learning and the fire handed to man by Prometheus, that which is already learned becomes stagnant and boring or useless, it is abstract knowledge such as the size of Pluto.

One of the questions that science is struggling with is that of the development of man, his cultures and beliefs in the past. All over the globe people are generally accepted as developing independent of each other.

Although this scientific stance that cultures from the Americas were independent of Europe and the native's cultures of south America for example are unlikely to have been influenced by the Egyptian religious concepts, despite the obvious pyramids found all over the world. The Sun god concepts and art and the idols that were created such archetypes as the *Mother Goddess* seemingly are shared between independent cultures. Legends such as the brothers, sons killing brothers found across the globe all suggest that man did influence man across continents, that Columbus may have found America in 1662, but the Egyptians of 4000BC somehow got there or vice-verse long before.

One of the greatest legends is that of the flood, which like the brothers/uncle legend which I presented as aspects of the

Lucifer archetype in *"Exegesis of Lucifer"*, these characters exists in every popular post creation legend in the world.

The Great flood as mentioned in the Bible, a book that the atheist will dismiss as irrelevant nonsense, was clearly a real worldwide event. The legend of Noah is just one

interpretation of a much, much older flood story and has the character and story under different names predating the supposed period of Noah by thousands of years, before even Zoroastrianism, clearly open for ridicule because of the notion of animals going in a boat, floating for forty-days and forty-nights, then land, then the second origins of all other men who descended now, not from Adam and Eve, but the sons of Noah.

Melišipak kudurru (Melišiḫuin)

Melišiḫuin was the 33rd king of the Kassite or 3rd Dynasty of Babylon circa 1186–1172 BC or Kassite

The above Babylonian tablet, clearly displays three significant entities in the sky, I believe the one on the left to be our sun, shown as always as it is today, the middle is the moon, you will take note of the under-earth curvature, reminiscent of the bull horns.

It is entirely possible that the bull horns in the middle is not a separate entity of *The Moon*, but a way of depicting the transition of the moon before the sun, *The Moon* is the object to the far right and the depiction is that of a solar eclipse and that the symbol in the centre is depicting when the two bodies crossed.

But, maybe to the right, a rival to the modern-day sun in terms of luminosity. Is this the Morning Star which collided with our sun, destroyed making people now observe Venus, the morning star and Lucifer the light bringer thinking it was the remnants?

Or due to its larger outer circle, is this the slightly dimmer aura of a near-distant supernova?

Our Astrological observation started as best we can tell with the Babylonians, who were excellent astronomers, aware of planetary movements, they simply would not depict anything this comparative to the sun and moon, in their sky unless there was an object that was comparable to be observed. But what this gives us is a very precise timescale for our investigation since Melišiḫuin ruled for just fifteen years to

1172BCE. Is this also the bright star that heralds the later told Bethlehem story?

In Genesis 1:3 God said Let there be light, we interpret that to be the creation of the sun in the biblical earth creation story, so why then does God create further light in Genesis 1:14 does god create further lights on day 3, but specifically in 1:16 it says "and god made two great lights; the greater one to rule the day and a lesser on with the stars to rule the night. We could assume that the lesser one is the moon. I'm not implying this is how these objects came about, my concern is with what man saw in the skies in ancient times.

Three entities again depicted in this image, but as you can see the Horned Moon image which I suggested could be an eclipse is on the far left, so it doesn't quite fit the model of the sun and moon meeting in the eclipse model I mentioned

above.

Victory Stele of Naram-Sin

The majority verdict is that the asteroid belt is a collection of matter that for one reason or another has not yet, or has completely failed to form a planet. Another equally likely but less supported theory is that it is the remnants of a planet that once was, but destroyed by a cosmic impact. There is no doubt that between creation of our solar system and now, all celestial bodies within it have collided with many items, many times, all with effects that at the time reflected the severity and forces at play, yet with the passage of time and its erosive nature, the evidence fades like the conclusive proof of the event which comparatively recently in comparison to the creation of the earth, wiped out the dinosaurs. We gather what little evidence we can find, and make a judgement call. This method, I do not decry, while pointing out its possible failings, I also say, it's the best information we have, and so is valid until proven otherwise.

In 2011 astronomer Phil Plait wrote in science journal [8]*Disco verer* We do know that rogue planets roam the galaxy, and they were almost certainly ejected in this manner, so the idea of a lost solar system planet isn't crazy," in relation to a computer simulation that suggests that Jupiter knocked a planet, completely out of our solar system. He went on to state "It's pretty well established that the outer planets have moved around a bit since the solar system formed, with a possibility that Uranus and Neptune even swapped places! But the models have a hard time explaining how this could've happened without Jupiter totally messing up the inner solar system. The models seem to indicate the orbits of Mars and Earth would not look at all as they do today if this were the case."

So, there's plenty of support in the world of astronomy that certainly planets collide, of course without doubt this also means that planets collide with stars, especially since stares seemingly form the most gravitas and central hubs of their respective solar systems. This is also true of Binary stars or even independent stars with their own respective solar system or not.

Professor Mark Morris of the University of California at Los Angeles in the Department of Physics and Astronomy says "When you see two stars colliding with each other, it depends on how fast they're moving. If they're moving at speeds like we see at the centre of our galaxy, then the collision is extremely violent. If it's a head-on collision, the stars get completely splashed to the far corners of the galaxy. If they're merging at slower velocities than we see at our neck

---

[8]http://blogs.discovermagazine.com/badastronomy/2011/11/16/did-jupiter-toss-a-giant-planet-out-of-the-solar-system/#.V8gZc3T2Yy8

of the woods in our galaxy, then stars are happier to merge with us and coalesce into one single, more massive object."

Equally like planets who also have varying densities and mass, occasion may dictate that the stars collide, one is threw out of place, and may escape a more dominant solar gravity from its adversary.

It is entirely possible that at some point, or on more than one occasion our very own solar system underwent some similar activity. Our only opponent to this principle so far, is that we have no evidence. But we can be certain based on what we know at this point in time, this most likely happened, our question is, did it happen after the earths formation, more importantly to be relevant to my particular area of interest, did it happen while intelligent life lived on earth?

If so, how would they explain it, or describe it if they even survived it? And if they didn't what evidence is there they even existed, or did they even live on Earth.

You see here, I go slightly off tangent. Because, while such a catastrophic event could've occurred, without much physical evidence remaining due to the extraordinary period of equilibrium of harmony restoring itself from an intergalactic chaos, we cannot say for certain that there was not possibly even the dinosaur's intelligent life on earth, or nearby in our solar system that there was not.

The "ancient aliens" theory has been around for a while, and I may cross over a few times into some of these findings, but only in so much as I want to be fairly open minded and comprehensive in my considerations.

But let's put it like this, if the earth has been covered in water for the estimated 4.4million years of its 4.5million year existent. Has undergone many extinction level events, it is entirely possible that jelly fish – like invertebrates couldn't have evolved a highly technological civilisation that we would never, ever likely find any evidence of, because, well as invertebrate jelly fish, there would be no bones or easily identifiable fossils, land life has only existed and adapted to our environment for the past half a billion years and look how far we have come in the past five-thousand. Imagine what underwater life could've evolved in its two billion before we ever crawled out as the earths first amphibians, long before apes. I'm not suggesting this happened exactly as I say, simply that "we wouldn't know if it did".

If during mankind's history there was either a greatly illuminated planet in our solar system or even a second star, that is no longer around then what physical evidence should we look for and how would our pre-cartographic ancestors relay the story through the generations?

Well, first we look at man's ability to relay information on the most basic scale, starting with when was it we first learnt to use language to communicate. I rely on the internet to collate this knowledge ready for you here.

You may notice I use Wikipedia a lot in certain references, and I know a lot of people dismiss Wikipedia as a reference pool, yet I am careful to only use Wikipedia which, incidentally I love, to relay popular opinion on things that are not in any way in dispute. It's not the central hub of infinite wisdom I know, but when used as a reference for simple things which are uncontroversial or not disputed, it's as good as the best encyclopaedia in the world, so don't dismiss its use off hand.

The Devil's Advocate

Many try to define what being a Luciferian is, I have tried myself many times only to discover alternate and completely plausible definitions from others who identify themselves as Luciferian.

Ultimately the underlying philosophy seems to be an egotistical desire to express one's thoughts as though they are the insightful wisdom from an expert who believes themselves to have the answers. And I am guilty of indulging this morally questionable vice.

As an exercise in this vice, here I am again, telling other Luciferians how to be a Luciferian, and thus assuming once again, I have the answers.

I state now and always, that I am no more qualified or greater in my Luciferian path than anyone else, even it can be said, the novice who may have just watched their first season of the TV show "Lucifer" and decided that wearing a black suit, being devilishly handsome, having inexhaustible self-confidence and carrying an English Accent is the firsts steps to becoming Luciferian. ~Incidentally I have all four of those traits, maybe they are correct.

In my interaction with the global Luciferian community, I find that those who agree with my notions and those who post ideals that I agree with, generally win my approval as being "real Luciferians". This reciprocal indulgence of shared ideals is generally how cults, religions, sets and human division begins. In all subjects, we become a selective-collective, promoting our concepts as the true "enlightened" path and begin to create ever increasing chasms of division towards others as each side evolve the specifics of what defines our groups.

If by chance any of you are only reading this as a passing interest in theological and occult study, and not because you have a vested interest in Luciferianism as a path for yourself to follow, then I'm afraid to tell you, you're already halfway there.

At its highest level, Luciferianism is the search for wisdom, nothing more.

It is not evil, it is not devil worship, and it doesn't have to even be the spiritual definition of your life, if you don't want it to be. You may be under the impression that Luciferianism is Satanism and in that matter, you would be both correct and incorrect. You see as part of the search for wisdom you must support it with a foundation of broad knowledge. Knowledge or Gnosis is simply bothering to learn about things that interest you, it doesn't have to be in-depth knowledge in a subject, if anything that would probably be a disadvantage, because not many people can become an expert in all things, and I find that knowing the general top-level overview of as many subjects as you can is more conducive to being Luciferian than having a doctorate in one or two subjects. Because your goal is not knowledge, trivia and intellect it is wisdom, knowledge is simply a tool for the wise to use. In our modern world, knowledge has been replaced by the internet, if I want to quote the fourth law of thermodynamics, I do not need to be an expert in it. I use the internet to support my argument, (if I'm quoting the forth law of thermodynamics then odds are I'm in an argument).

What cannot be googled, is wisdom. Wisdom cannot be found in immediately available reference sources like books or the internet, you cannot cheat or pretend in a Facebook argument that you are wise if you are not. You can pretend if you like, to have a Ph.D. in astrophysics if you're good with google and a quick reader. And so suddenly, the world is filled with pseudo-physicists.

Is wisdom superior to knowledge?

This is another subjective question, my thoughts are a wise person can get by outside his natural domain by understanding how things work, even though he has never experienced this "thing" before. A knowledgeable person, will succeed better than a wise person, if the "thing" is something he is knowledgeable on, but face with a "thing" he is unfamiliar with, he will fail entirely.

Satanism under its original terms was one of those above-mentioned chasms created between a sect of Hebrew Monotheistic philosophers who considered, like we do, the purpose of life, its origins, why we have reason and the purpose of that reasoning? They concluded a perfectly reasonable philosophy with the support of the growing knowledge of mankind's understanding thus far, they continued to study the stars, motion, laws of nature and resolved some of the greatest questions mankind would ever face, with it would seem heavy influence from the Hellenic period of the Greeks. Some of it could not be proven, some was observable science and some was purely conjecture, all the ingredients of a well-structured religion, but like all theories, it remains valid until conclusively unproven with time.

Where it went wrong, and where even to this day it is still going wrong is; they created the oldest of all chasms between men. They defined a set of rules around these expanding ideas and philosophies. They wrote them down and literally "set them in stone", and from that point decided anyone who wished to expand upon, question or change these ideas were "the adversary", in Hebrew it is written *Ha-setan*, which later evolved into the word Satan, it simply means "those who are not like us" or "an opponent"," not in our group". So today, anything you believe, study or question which is outside of these ancient "laws of existence" is done by those who are contrary to their group. These acts of questioning or alternative theories are "satanic" and the people who spiritually define themselves outside the "club" become Satanists.

This book of laws later went on to become the Old Testament to the Western world. People who did not follow this path were "Demonised" called worshipers of "Satan", you may be surprised to find that "The New Testament" is Satanic under its original definition, however The New Testament, The Kabbalah and the Quran. All became subsets of this Abrahamic Lawbook, so they, despite being modern day adversaries, tend not to go so far as to identify each other as Satanic. They have enough population outside their cults to label as Satanic.

Of course, within the adversarial faiths there then becomes a group of people who revel in the fact that they reject this philosophy of the ancient Hebrews. These anti-heroes identify with the satanic nature of man and the freedom from dogma this provides, they fully endorse its darker and rebellious nature to the mechanism which is used to enslave those who wish to be devout followers of any theistic cult.

These people form extreme end of the spectrum of what comes under a satanic philosophy. Science, astrology, astronomy, seeking to further mankind's understanding of the universe all at some point have been labelled "heresy" at some point in man's history.

So is Luciferianism Satanic, yes, by the Hebrew definition which we base our current interpretation from. But then so is looking in the mirror or praying to Jesus before God himself.

Under what I like to call the "Hollywood" definition which indulges in horror movies and sinister demons, for the most case and for most people's understanding of Satanic, Luciferianism is not, well my version of it is not at least.

If Luciferianism is wisdom, then you must know what wisdom is, and "in my opinion", wisdom is "not having an opinion" as paradoxical as that may be. While I may be Luciferian in principle, it's a path, a lifestyle and a choice, and by being a choice I step in and out of my Luciferian mask as I see fit.

We begin realising that opinion and subjective viewpoints are invalid in the grand scheme of states of matter. The last thing Luciferianism is, would be "hating people" or "hating another religion" because a Luciferian realises that a person's faith is nothing more than a subjective opinion. A Luciferian engages with an adversary, listens and learns from what they believe, to expand the debate a Luciferian will often present alternate viewpoints from other beliefs and sees how the argument stands up.

With this new knowledge, he will do the same with yet another, and another until ultimately, he has a balanced set of arguments that he finds "enlightening", and he has dismissed all the others that have fallen against opposing argument from his sources.

A Luciferian is, I believe the evolution of man in his Aquarian Aeon, it is the literal "natural selection by survival of the fittest". By taking the knowledge and beliefs of one person and then taking opposing beliefs of another, without his own subjective influence clouding his judgement he can dismiss that which is not true, or doesn't hold water. He can share the greater and more valid arguments, and thus ensuring the survival of true knowledge, spirituality and light. He becomes the light bringer for future generations.

Lucifer the character is often defined as the devil, yet he is the original morning star, heralding the dawn, bringing illumination to the forthcoming day which brings new knowledge and does not lock us in the past to superstition and dogma, he is the symbol of enlightenment, rebellion from chains of moral and dogmatic slavery, he exists in all of us if we wish it to be.

> I do find that so many people misunderstand my Luciferianism and see me as argumentative, and they could not be more wrong "he argues".

The fact is I am not trying to convince people my point of view, often you will find you cannot, unless they too are very wise. What I am doing is questioning theirs, vigorously maybe, but I am trying to learn, using arguments that I have found most valid thus far. If I find my argument does not hold water, I am not disappointed, believe me I am ecstatic, this was my goal. Surprisingly this has had me kicked out of a few Luciferian groups on the internet, who see any questioning of their beliefs in the same way as the ancient Hebrews, and thus expelled me from their sect, "the greater church of Lucifer" being one, ironic isn't it. Of course, I put that down to probably one individual who "walks the walk, but cannot talk the talk".

The Satan Concept

There are as many visions of Satan as there are minds creating those visions. Maybe even more since many of the people who begin to invest their time in exploring the greater spiritual self, from any spiritual path will have some aspect of opposition to their core values. By reading this I assume you are one such person, who has defined what Satan represents to you. Thus, every person has their personal Satan, and you may be like me know that to define Satan is a perilous path to get a consensus.

That Satan may not just be one iconic figurehead as often represented by the horned gods of pagan culture, he may me represented of your freedom or true will, or could be your personal or group adversaries.

Reject or embrace him I wanted to pass on an often-overlooked gnostic aspect, which oft gets overshadowed by the more modern demonic icon.

One of the stronger themes through my books is that of the duality or dichotomy of the whole of the individual. You and me, we're made up of two distinct and separate entities which is the cornerstone of 4th century gnostic codices.

I have gone into much more detail many times in the past so for the benefit of my frequent readers I will skip that and simply say "we are made of matter and spirit" and these present the dichotomy which is the topic of almost all religious teachings, mysticism, occult and can be extended to the greater universe, energies, light & darkness, push and pull. You name it, it's there.

And the overlooked aspect I wanted to talk about is that aspect of master and servant.

Master, is in family of the word 'Aster, Astro, Star, stellar,' and like the stars, heavenly, aloft, above. In a relationship, we will naturally place a master above a servant and those that master things effectively become the "lords" of those under them. It is associated with the air in the four base elemental symbols Air, Earth, Fire & Water.

Servant, is in the phonetic family of the serpent, the snake on its belly, a much-grounded thing. In true opposition for our dichotomy the servant is earth. It represents the physical, the carnal.

And in the purest order of the Christian Gnostic's the mind, thought, reason should be the master of the physical, the body. Our nearest star, The Sun, which ultimately evolved into the symbol for the one god of heaven even for the Christian faith, is our lord and master. He is in the air, and to be as divine, we must be as that master, commanding from the mind and resisting the carnal pleasures. That's not just sex, in the case of chastity often practiced by Holy orders, religious sects and belief systems around the world, it manifests itself in things like fasting's, Ramadan, self-flagellation. In the seeds of all these systems in the rejection of the physical.

This leads us each to our personal dichotomy, which is embraced by the philosophical versions of Luciferianism and Satanism. We realise that we are a composite of the two aspects of body and mind or spirit to distinguish the ethereal though which makes us who we are, from the physical lump of grey-stuff in our cranial cavity.

The acceptance of this is really the heart of modern Satanistic concepts, not so much the Devil worship that historical religious zealots would imbue on anyone that they labelled "adversary" to their personal political gain.

The Devil himself, an icon is fictitious. We in our modern times have been handed a mythology by irrational people, listening to the rhetoric of manipulation masters for hundreds of years. Men in power, with armies whipping up the illiterate yokels and townsfolk into conformity or eternal damnation. Worship Jesus or burn forever in Hell.

All rational people now know better. This dogmatic and forced belief from any religion ultimately will bring about a hatred for it. Which is a damn shame, because despite what most people think, I for one, and I know many others which call themselves Luciferian can happily embrace the Gnostic teachings, even from the 4th century Catholics. Because what we interpret it as today, is tainted with 1500 years of distortion. But it was distortion for good reason.

The philosophies and theologies that were the original teachings became heretical and so the preservation of them created the nonsense that is now taken literally. This creates fools of both the Christians, Islamists and Jews, who worship it as fact, and the opposer's, including Luciferians, Satanists and Atheists who equally have literally interpret it to claim it as nonsense.

It is truth, corrupted. It is metaphors, philosophy, symbology, astrology and yes, ancient science. And it's our duty to discover it, for the matter of historical accuracy and find out what was meant originally by our ancestors and each stage of that dilution of intent that lead us to where we are today. We need to know what we have forgotten, and for the sake of humanity, truth.

While we take the side of literal belief or abstract rejection we are doing mankind a disservice.

One of the things lost on our modern minds is concept of mastery, mastery of our own body.

You may well think that you are master of your own mind, and that your mind does all the work, because this is where we are today in knowing our physiology. You must remember though that things have not always been "thought of" this way. What is an impulse or an instinct, where is it driven from? When you are hungry, does your mind tell your belly? Or does your belly tell your mind?

Now if you're like me, I think it's a case that my belly tells my mind. And I'm no doctor but I would guess that the sensation is some nerves passing data to my mind. But what is my mind? Is that nerves? From ancient man's point of view the heart ached, the belly rumbled these are methods of communication. They are equally intelligent to whatever signals the mind sends to the body to tell it to move. The body as a whole was sentient, maybe less sentient than the head in terms of the brain would be used for reasoning. But the body is a whole organic organ that was in equal regard.

So even the brain itself, would not then, nor does it now count as spirit, soul or the essence of you, it's just another organ.

And if the stomach, is telling the spirit "you're hungry, eat now" who is the master? Clearly the Servant. The serpent, Kundalini, the spine, the phallus, and the flesh is mastering the spirit (the father), the natural order of heavenly worship.

This is literally overturning the cross (an adopted satanic symbol), and so to the Gnostic Catholics and varying religious orders ever since the concepts of moral behaviour were created. Indulging Satan in their purist sense of the faith is giving in to the simplest bodily needs. Today we recognise bodily urges as being a part of the solistic self, and not in any way an evil opposite to our spiritual minds. The resultant carnal pleasures which became regarded as sinful were things such as exposing the body itself, sex, eating excessively, masturbation, dancing, drinking, tattooing, and vanity.

Effectively, anything that gives your body more consideration than your mind is sinful. This mind-set is why, according to even modern-day Catholicism, we are still "born in sin", although not many know the reason why we are to blame for a sinful sexual act of our parents, the spoken belief that this is true, is re-iterated blindly to this day, such is the power of these thousands of years old ideologies.

The little understood concept of repenting or going to purgatory for simply being born baffles most, but I will share it with you. The concept is, that we as spirit exist, prior to being born. The ritual act of sex between our parents engaged in sinful activity, indulging their flesh. Out of holy sanction especially, or done gratuitously, is a magical act to summon forth the "pure" spirit of you, innocent and "astral". Tempted by experiencing the flesh, you respond to the summoning and are born to indulge in a life of its pleasures. Therefore, you have sinned simply by being born, as you were not considered uncooperative to the actions.

The Air is as opposed to the Earth as the Water is to the Fire. One is considered creative, water, which brings life, fire destroys. Water is therefore in simplistic gnostic sense good, and fire is bad. Where it all went wrong is some patriarchal political sects began idealising that this dichotomic concept represented good and evil, but this was not the original intent of the philosophy which predated written records. When we apply this division to all aspects of the universe we can place ourselves on one side or the other. We can

be master or slave, it was clearly considered better to be a master, masters became nobles, and nobles became kings. Slaves on the other hand, well they became bad, and so ill-treatment, punishment and disregard evolved into the mind-set that punishing your slave was substitute for punishing the flesh, of yourself, slaves were considered cattle, equally valid for sacrifice, as were women, who were represented as the earth aspect of this dichotomy. A battle some women still fight to this day and presented itself in the bible, by Eve, temptress and temped by the serpent. Lilith, bearing infinite demons.

So why pick on the Serpent as the symbol of evil. Snakes, only later were considered a cursed animal. If upon the arrival of an all-powerful monadic, creator god specifically identified as a sky god, or aspect of sun worship, he then cursed them to crawl on their bell. They could never aspire to be anything more than a snake, no limbs, no wings, they are as close to earth as you can get.

The earth itself, land represented the physical aspects of life itself. Water, where it spread through the land would bring life, agriculture. In the humid dessert lands, establishments would form where there was a water supply. Since there were no discernible features to the Snake other than their phallus shape, they could for the later evolution which drifted from a more balanced view in favour of the more dominant sky gods, considered without spirit (air), simply moving in perpetuum as material (earth) and carnal states of consumption. As that is all they effectively could do.

For some gnostic sects, the feet were representative of the earth nature of man. Leading to the sayings of "feet of clay"

or "cold feet". The feet of the living man, touched the earth. It opposed his highest spiritual self. Others considered the base of the spine, the anus as the negative aspect.

This could well be the purpose of the symbolism behind the Abraxas (ΑΒΡΑΣΑΞ) a go, with bird head, and snake legs, showing the opposing earth and air symbols. If we consider the Sumerian eagle and wind creatures being representative of the "heavenly" gods, then the snake represents the earthly ones, and intended not as a negative representation they later came to denote, but ones met with equal admiration. The Abraxas figure has the cock (head), the human intermediary (body) and the snake (legs).

Luciferianism's Relationship to Satanism.

To start this discourse, there are two primary versions of Satan which we must define to distinguish between. The first is the pronoun 'satan' followed by the proper noun 'Satan' the aspect or entity.

We start with the defining of *satan* by researching its original meaning. "Ha Satan" is an ancient word which is used in the Bible to refer to the adversary.

Since biblical times, its translation and its concepts are usually the western world's first encounter with this *satan* concept. The definition intended from this source is most pertinent to our understanding of it and our purpose of the word.

This biblical use for our purpose forms our original conceptual definition of the now evolved proper noun "Satan" which we embody as a demonic entity and adversary to the monotheistic 'God' of the bible. In its original use, it is a generic word which encapsulated quite a few meanings depending on the context it was used in. It was a subjective condition under its original definition to a third-person plural personal pronoun.

In modern language, possibly its closest English word would be "them". But seemingly with a twist since "them" in English is quite passive and does not infer any feeling or description of how we are to view "them". It doesn't necessarily follow that the "them" in question are thought of with any negative connotations. Ha~satan however it would seem, does. Seemingly it has an influence of bitterness or caution towards the party in question. In English, I believe we have replaced this expression by a scowl in our eyes while using the word "them" to indicate a "them" with a degree of disdain.

Ha~satan under this definition is female word gender, as Ha~satan is the feminine form of the word SitNah which is commonly aligned with the word 'The Resistance' or 'The Rebellion'. This gender opposition is indicative of the patriarchal nature of the Bible.

The word itself is made up from Hebrew text 'Nun Tet Shin' which in its original form is written שטן in Hebrew, unlike English, Hebrew is read from right to left so we would phonetically write it Shin-Tet-Nun. Whose individual characters convey many meanings.

Shin, is consumption, it devours and eats all in its path, it is the opposing destroyer which all things created ultimately succumb to.

Tet, is Aligned with a Snake, to wrap, to wind, it surrounds and is the darkness which any light is surely engulfed in.

Nun, is like the more common but not western word 'Chi' but I think most of you will understand it, it can mean Life, Eternity or Flow, perpetually in motion.

So *satan* is and will always be open to interpretation, but the connotations show why we perceive Satan as the serpent enticing Eve to eat from the apple in the garden of Eden.

Ha~satan has been aligned with many modern words such as "our adversary" or "the accuser", although personally I think this to mean more correctly translated to 'the retributer' or my personal favourite "That which is not us" which to more correctly defines its relationship with the subject, in that it is a description of people who do not hold our values, or are not like us.

Conceptually we can from this perceive *satan* is an eternal devourer of life, which brings us as always to the importance of the symbol of Ouroboros, the eternal consuming snake. As a dynamic opposition to creation, the figurehead of all that must be consumed is synonymous with death as a concept. Death is unrelentingly and eternally consuming life. Making *satan* a thing that we, as living people are not, something we fear, the enemy that will always be coming to consume us. Not only our own life, but all that we hold dear, our family, our values, all that we believe to be good. Therefore, *satan* is the epitome of the evil enemy.

Satanists have embraced this name as a testimony to being adversarial to the dogma of religious piety.

Using this definition, as its original purpose Ha~satan could in theory be used by someone who identifies himself as a Satanist, towards a Christian, because subjectively the Christian is ha~satan to the philosophy of the Satanists. And Ironically, it is therefore impossible to call yourself a Satanist, in the same way it is impossible to describe yourself as "someone not like me". But in another way, we are all ha~satan from another's adversarial point of view.

The definition of Satan in one form or another then, has been used many times in the bible and books that deal with subjective values towards a disliked or feared opponent for as long as we have been able to demonstrate civilised culture.

This definition created the demonization of so many pagan gods which would be considered *satan* to our earliest documentation originating from our modern middle east and the birthplace of Abrahamic and other Sun worship religions. Even European sun worship religions were engulfed in this wave of tribalism which as religion always does, serves more to divide than to unite, which is disappointing since the word "religion" actually means unite.

As time has passed Satanists primarily became the collective name for none conformists to the Judeo-Christian movement, they were considered evil and worshipers of devils or "the devil" whose etymological evolution has followed a similar vein. We realise a distinction between "the Devil" and "devils" The Devil later became synonymous with our second definition of the proper noun of Satan.

Satan became an iconic figurehead of all those pagan gods (I use pagan here under its definition of gods that are non-Abrahamic). This concept of ha~satan like other conceptual states of being became characterised with a figurehead, an artificial icon portrayed in art and literature to be a single embodiment of those collective gods, a single figurehead to represent all evil opponents to the subjective views of the Abrahamic faith.

This has led to much confusion over the years, where some of these pagan and other gods or demigods, particularly the ones which have a darker or fearful attribute representation were adopted as being minions of this Satan character. Asmodeus,

Pan, Beelzebub, Baphomet often got artistically depicted with similar features of the goat, horned and cloven hoofed, to unite them as pertinent to sinful pursuits.

But it didn't stop there, there was the period of the dark days of the first millennium, the growing Christian church murderously spread its geopolitical influence north into Europe from its base in Rome taking and corrupting the original peaceful message of the New Testament and enforcing it with the doom and damnation from the Old Testament as a punishment for non-conformation .

These evil power mad ranks perverted the peaceful message of the meek, it into a forced doctrine to manipulate kings and possess a sickening amount of power and wealth which tore apart the complex and mixed faiths of the northern European beliefs.

Turning their nature based pagan religions into what they would call "Devils work", the Satan character evolved from in the later 18th Century. And so, Satan the new name for the king of Hell was born, from the minds of the evil Catholic Church whose goals were the manipulation of man, obtaining of wealth and political influence to control the known world, not as a country, or an army but as a virtual state undefined by monarchical and geographical borders.

Piety was their banner and they would enact the most evil and diabolical torture to those who did not declare fidelity to their command, in the name of their modernised version of the ancient and indeed pagan Sun God, Horus. Son of Osiris, the King of the sky in Egyptian mythology, rebranded under the name Jesus, son of the one true god.

Thankfully now, Christians are becoming more tolerant of other faiths, and fundamental Christians are a dying breed as the word of the new testament, its good intentions can be read by a greater educated populous. As Luciferians, we should explore any gnosis we can benefit from it, and not take the subjective view of those that pedal it.

Historically the interpretation of the bible and its selective passages was assigned to a few scholars who assembled the communal flock on their holy Sun-day and condemned the flock to certain death and eternal damnation if they strayed from the manipulation of the church syllabus.

Satan would take their souls, and burn them in fire and brimstone, and anyone who did not conform to the doctrine of the church were worshipers of Satan. Pagan rituals, other godly prayers in any form were aligned with devil worship, "evil" and the work of Satan, including the bellum sacrum (Holy War) we call the crusades before the Muslim God was adopted into the fold of monotheistic alignment with the Christian God under its Abrahamic umbrella. Satanic practice for a long while included medicine and the sciences. The syllabus was that faith above all, and that Gods will should always be done (being the churches version of God's will). Anything out-with the direct teachings of the church was satanic. This was the extent of their paranoia and manipulative ego to maintain a firm grip on our lives.

Time, like the recursive consuming snake of ha~satan waits for no man, and the era of Catholicism under its old guise is thankfully all but destroyed, it has nominal influence politically any more, much like the monarchy, whose greed went hand in hand. It retains some wealth and influence, but lacks any real power since the reformation, which divided the allegiance between the monarchy, state and church, and significantly displayed to the common man, that the divided power in conflict meant we on an individual level could choose a personal allegiance, yet not be instantly condemned by the aligned forces, due to the protection from the opposing faction's governments, monarchies or church. Modern days, people are more able to embrace other religions according to their personal convictions rather than one forced upon them in most civilised countries. Sadly, there is still a few rogue nations or idealist forces who pathetically think that true faith can be forced upon people and use their geo-political or military influence to somehow make people conform to their beliefs under punishment of stoning or other such torture. These fundamentalists will die out like the inquisitional Catholics and all other such fundamental ideologists. Saying that, it is not on my part ever to criticise any faith itself, no only the fundamentalists that seek to force their faith onto anyone else. Their whole concept is a farce, and they are idiots. Faith surely, to be true is found within and conceived from will, or it is worthless. Any professing of a faith that is coerced by fear is not true faith, surely under that premise the fundamentalists have lost before they begin.

Rome seem to have captured the market on dictation of beliefs from the times of their significant expansion of the Roman Empire. The Roman gods historically seem to have been used iconically more than any other. Lucifer is no exception. Lucifer iconically is the Romano-Pagan god of wisdom which is defined is personal illumination. Thus, any form of light can be identified as being a reflection or embodiment of the concept of Lucifer. Ancient sciences such as cosmology, philosophy, physics and chemistry all fall under the category of gnosis, which means knowledge in Greek.

Lucifer being a pagan god of wisdom and incorporating the sciences and philosophy was collimated into the satanic concept. Science would produce effects that could be considered magical in nature, and nature itself would not produce the effects of science alone. It was only when he applied knowledge, man could predict heavenly movements, create fire, cure illness and advance a technical civilization that was a creation of man, aspiring to be as God. And he did this by building upon his library of knowledge with experiments and treatments.

Writing and recording these experiments lead to a few scholars proposing what was considered by the church to be a blasphemous idea. Such heresy as the heliocentric solar system, saving lives that God's will had marked for death, and creation itself was according to fundamental Christians the Devil's,. Practitioners of these crafts were known as wizards, which means wise-men and they were Satanists simply because they were considered adversaries to the church. Being a Romano-Pagan symbol of these arts, Lucifer quickly rose in ranks of some imaginary demonic hierarchy according to the Christians. Lucifer became more than simply one of the many figureheads that they believed to be devils, and aligned him with the figurehead Satan himself. Therefore, many in modern day many people, including Satanists and Luciferians consider Lucifer to be iconically Satan. Based on my opinions you have been reading, I conclude that he is not, but I can understand why so many people think so.

We are now in an age where people can easily identify themselves as being "Satanists" contrary to my above explanation. Words evolve and so the new definition is more valid than the old, because words are intended to convey meaning, and their meaning is not determined by a book, or history, but it is ultimately determined not by what the greater populous perceive they mean.

Satanist today are prepared to reject the Abrahamic faiths dogma to the extent that they will identify with the adversary. Some will embrace the demonic culture and its dark fashion. Some will go to the extreme of embracing its conceptually "evil" nature, but in my opinion they have not freed themselves from the definition proposed by Christianity as they still allow it to define who they are, by regarding the Christian imposed definition to define them.

Luciferianism is a branch of Satanism, which continues under the icon of the morning star, illuminating our way to gnosis, we follow that star in the east, like the wise men to find the birth of our own christos-conciousness (you see there is meaningful parables in the Bible if you know how to read it). I don't claim to be a scientist in any way, bar the passing interest that stems from simply wishing to understand the nature of myself, who I am and where I come from on a conscious level, which transcends into a physical level. But saying that Satanism, like paganism is a collective term for many beliefs and paths. There are as many devil worshipers as there are Atheists, Satanism has now evolved into a third definition thanks to Anton LaVey which is indulgence in the power and responsibility of oneself. The buck stops here, they answer to no higher authority, it embraces the rejection of any god, and thus fits nicely under the definition of the original ha~satan from the Abrahamic point of view. Modern Satanism also aligns with the modern Luciferian, who has chosen the identity of "I am God" which is also a concept of many definitions. No longer content with simply being a man of wisdom or of the arts, but a Satanist who can either believe mankind to be the pinnacle of consciousness in his known universe, or as I, a gnostic Luciferian who believes that I am a part of a living god.

Of course, all things are subjective, I can only share my current understanding of truth. It is a complex topic, where the boundaries of Satan, Satanism, Lucifer and Luciferianism, even Paganism do not have clear definitions. This is why we struggle to propose a single ideal when discussing the many topics of the occult theology, much like astrology we cannot simply take a planet and what house it lies in as an absolute representation of its meaning. Its relationship and transitions to other astrological aspects define its meaning in that context, you then take from that the subjective parallels in your own life and try to make sense of it.

I certainly have not covered all the subjective concepts of any of the principles here. In fact, with several blogs and three books (soon to be four) on theologian concepts I have hardly touched the surface of even Luciferianism, let alone the spectrum and relationship to Satanism or even Christianity.

Lucifer is the symbol of light, illumination, the seeking of betterment of ourselves and our relationship with the universe.

Understanding Gnostic Symbolism.

Possibly the greatest leap for me towards the goal of enlightenment was not so much a single fact or message, but the realization of the symbolic nature of historic texts. So, I thought I should try to explain it as best I can, because there really is no hard and fast rule which you can apply to any specific word or codex. But once you start interpreting gnostic holistic values in such ways it certainly means these biblical parables which read literal nonsense, have some meanings that you realise are very heretical compared to the literal bible teachings. Which leads you to respect aspects of the bible.

At first, I used to, like most rational people, not think the bible was literal, I can't say I ever leaped into atheism. I have always been a little spiritual, and like most just thought the bible was written by an undeveloped civilisation, making gods of things that they didn't understand. I believed that we have advanced, were superior and clearly more developed than some two thousand year of sandal wearing camel jockeys. I now believe I couldn't have been more wrong, while we have advanced greatly in the material half of human's complex, we have disregarded our spiritual nature which has been perceived as an unworthy pursuit which realises little material gain. And that is the exact point of our loss, we see no material gain in the study of something that is without material substance, it will never have material substance, no more than materialism will have ever, any spiritual substance. You could say it's a similar gratification to payday lending, we want instant results, change, proof, gratification and they are presented only in the physical reward.

I believe the historic ancestors were highly advanced in an equal balance of the material and spiritual universe, but at some point, in the past, seeing the instant gratification of material endeavour we left the less obvious spiritual nature behind. Unfortunately, the sudden drop of a developed spiritual aspect of our whole was not immediately filled by the material and technological advancement that rewarded so presently and this created what we now call "the dark ages". We crawled out of those dark ages, purely on the will and industry of man using the material side of our whole. Creating gain, but an imbalance. It is a shame, a great shame that the two were not nurtured equally, symbiotically feeding each other, we certainly would be a lot more advance than we are now.

The above chart shows what I'm trying to explain in terms of golden era enlightenment, where rather than enemies, the spiritual nature of man and the physical combine to make a whole, achieved, enlightened individual. The blue line shows our spiritual understanding of the universe, not any religious doctrine and deference to god, which has been the most destructive force against spirituality than anything else. Its spirituality itself, the age-old question of why am I here, what's it all about, how significant is my reason in the universe, which in the ancient times of the great philosophers was highly advanced, hence the arbitrary score of "6" units of wonderfulness I have given it. The Red line shows where we were technologically, taking advantage of the material resources of the world and our understanding of the nature pf physics as a science. You can see although low, 3,000 years ago it is what it is. We had fire, metals, alloys and wheels. A good solid platform to establish civilisation and so worthy of 1 point of wonderfulness. The grey line is simply the two states of the holistic man, his spiritual nature and his material nature combined. And the yellow, golden era, is where the ideal should be, where material and spiritual combine and grow at similar rates. And what I'm trying to allude to is that, rather than being at odds to each other, where one side of the coin must be destroyed so that the other may grow, is false. It hurts us holistically, we should seek to grow both, and the ages where we achieve this, this promised coming age of Aquarius, can only be achieved by spiritual growth, we need not fight technology with spirituality, that would be no beneficial than the effects back in 1000 ad when the advent of imposed religion, heresy of the sciences brought about a dark age.

The Principles of Change.

If we believe that each and every individual desires a better life, not just for himself but for all mankind. People as a whole are not innately explicitly selfish. The desire of the individual is formed in increasing circles of selfishness, but the term selfishness is often, like our mascot and light-bearer maligned without due consideration.

self·ish
/ˈselfiSH/

adjective

(of a person, action, or motive) lacking consideration for others; concerned chiefly with one's own personal profit or pleasure.
"I joined them for selfish reasons"
synonyms: egocentric, egotistic, egotistical, egomaniacal, self-centered, self-absorbed, self-obsessed, self-seeking, self-serving, wrapped up in oneself; More

As Luciferians, many of our precepts relate around those of self-discovery, self-exploration and self-realisation. In short, the "self".

And simple word structure of "self-ish" without its negative connotations is to be considered the considerations of a self-centric universe. We are, and all consciousness is self-centric. Metaphysically our universe is made of matter that orbits around our conscious subjective selves. Reality is self-centric unless we are considering abstraction or empathic considerations of external entities.

In this sense, we are entities of the self "selfish" by nature. Unless we are the great universal consciousness which is all things, which for the time being, we are not.

So, let us indulge our selfish realities, to explore ourselves.

Our primary survival instinct is selfish. This is a progressive part of our survival system, it is for all innate and unchanging as a primitive instinct. We of course can reason to countermand this primordial directive by conscious determination such as suicide or more immediate for any parents out there, conscious sacrifice on behalf of a loved one. But that does not mean that the primordial directive of selfish survival wasn't there as an instinct before our determined relegation of that command. It just means it was superseded.

The primordial survival instinct existed before you gained awareness of such concepts as sacrifice or suicide and so must remain higher in the pyramid of self-centrism. We are the centre of our universes regardless of physical location and our subjective centre moves around with us.

What comes next is our possessions, and possessions for this discussion are all things that we have a possessive value to. Now I want to speak frankly, and I know my intended audience of enlightened folk do not want to "beat around the bush" with pointless explanations to cater for the socially acceptable PC brigade. It goes without saying, especially to Luciferians that people are not possessions. But in terms of what relationships really are in concept is establish possession of a bond between to people. You may not own the person, but you own the bond, or maybe a better term would be to share a bond. But that would imply the bond is mutual, and in the case of a stalker to his prey, the relationships bond is far from a mutual arrangement. The same with unrequited love.

So, with that in mind we all possess an individual bond which forms the relationship we have towards others.

Ad so in that context, and to save having to explain all individual relationships on a case by case basis. I will simply say I "own" possessively "my children", "my wife", "my friends", and "my readers "(you). And I expect you should understand what that means without taking offence.

The next relationship of possession is the extend of that bond, thus dictates the level to which our selfishness extends. If we consider wealth as a medium of this bond, we rational folk would usually extend our desire for wealth to map itself nicely over our selfish relationship technology.

While we all desire world wealth, an end to poverty and a fair distribution of wealth as a principle, it is primarily "selfish" in the way we are prepared to distribute our own portion of that wealth. Like sacrifice, instinctually we place ourselves at highest consideration, and like our sacrifice of survival which we may throw ourselves into the flames to save loved ones as a theoretical principle, while we think we may give our children our last pennies in principle, we don't perceive wealth as terminal as life, so we are more cautious in our approach to it. We consider ourselves probably wiser custodians of the wealth than those we are prepared to imbue with it.

The finality of mortality in self-sacrifice defines that since we no longer need life, it is easier to part with life in theory, than it is to part with wealth, as if we forgo our wealth entirely, we are not faced with the finality of death and so must make provisions. We are more likely to give our lives to our children than we are our "real" last penny.

Of course, any (not extremely wealthy) parent has gone without money for a while to finish their child with something they feel is essential to their continued progress in life. But we usually do that with the cushion that given next pay day "I'll be okay again". It's unlikely we literally give our last penny until we are terminally leaving the physical world. Were merely give our last current resource of wealth.

So, this shows, despite our claims of "I would give my life for my kids", we still hold selfish caveats to our conceptual idealism.

Power Word "Amen"

It is almost unbelievable that this ancient word of magick has been so embraced by the Christian collective. But as always this is simply a testament to how the church has corrupted the original hermetic truth of the Christian faith to nothing more than sheep following a shepherd mentality.

So, as much for the benefit of true Christians hoping to find the gnostic truths behind their religion, instead of the mass mind control that we now have in the 21st Century. I have decided to share with you the real and from a Christians point of view "Satanic" meaning of the power word "Amen".

I have no issue with satanic positions on things, using my definition of Satanism, which can be found in my other posts. To that extent, I won't bother repeating that which I have emphasised many times before. Being Luciferian, we accept all aspects of spectral existence as a real concept from which we can learn, and to shun any knowledge or philosophy out of hand is to be blinkered and ill-informed. You must closely examine madness to know what is sanity.

Amen, in the modern sense is a root Hebrew word that means the same as the wiccan, or pagan "so-mote-it-be". It was adopted as part of Christian ceremony or ritual prayer as the conclusion to spell craft was expected in the northern European pagan regions. On adoption of Christianity, the transition needed to be metered as to not cause confusion. I will not go into premise regarding the political motives of Constantine which are well documented for those that are interested. Suffice to say, pagan communities were heavily influenced into adopting the Christian faith and so many concepts were aligned to smooth the transition.

The phrases "so-be-it" or "so-may-it-be" are a declaration of will, specifically the will of the spell caster. And as un-satanic as that may sound to a rational mind, we have to look into the irrational mind of the fundamentalist- Abrahamicist, such as Christian, Jew, or Muslim. The three main faiths that share the monotheistic Abrahamic based Bible, Torah or Quran.

You see, in the Abrahamic mono-theistic law system that these religions adhere to, God's will is paramount, and man is subject only to God's law and will. Fair enough, this is why we have some fundamentalist Abrahamicists who refuse medical intervention and blood transfusions.

Because they put all their faith in the power of god, even to the point of self-harm, or indeed to the demise of their loved ones. In their beliefs man has no place to demand of God their personal will. Yet the conclusion of a prayer with the word "Amen" is doing exactly that, it is telling God, "make this happen" and therefore is not a prayer, but is actually a casting, since the will is issued from the individual rather than God. By definition a casting is to "form into material", you can cast metal, you can cast a net, where the net is emitted from the caster, it is something that comes from a person rather than received.

What an Abrahamic prayer should end with based on their absolute submission to God's will, is more similar to the request, "if it be gods will". By ending this way, you are expressing a desire to God, but not demanding it, making the preceding list of desires a prayer, rather than a casting.

The resulting English word Amen or Muslim Ameen, has been part of an amalgamation of languages, all with similar root meaning who finds its origins in the Middle East and northern African territories. As with most of our religious words it is heavily influenced by Hebrew, Aramaic and Greek.

In Hebrew it is the combination of Aleph, Mem and Nun letters "AMN" which can be read as aman, amon and amen. The subtleties in its vowel-less interpretations, although specifically different rely on the context in which it was presented to indicate definition. Regionally it is pronounced either "Ay-Men" or "Ahr-Men".

Some hope can be given to its Abrahamic usage, in that it can be interpreted to mean "have faith" or "believe". Yet still, "believe" can also take it into a satanic usage, in that to "believe" is a part of the manifestation of will which is prevalent in modern satanic crafting, often presented under many new-age names such as "law of attraction" and mesmerism, which rose at the same time as spiritualists and theosophy movements in the nineteenth and twentieth century. In particular to this, the works of Phineas Quimby's new-thought movement.

Be-live, is to command something into action. The movement shares many Luciferian and theosophical concepts, such as the divinity which is emitted from or shared by man and God, rather than received from an exclusive and externalised. These principles later evolved into varying occultists and often considered satanic branches, not least of which became the OTO, Golden Dawn and the works of Alistair Crowley.

"Have faith" is their strongest argument for its use, as it would imply a trust in their god to see things right for them. But this is tenuous, when all the other definitions are implied as command rather than request. Especially when one does not define in its usage as to who we are to have faith in? In fact it probably should read the same as "believe", as you are in fact commanding God to do your will, a wholly adversarial principle to the absolute trust in "Gods will" and a method of spell-craft associated with the Djinn, and the summoning of demons to act on your behalf.

It is posited that the word "amen" also stems from the Egyptian God "Amun" or "Amun-Ra", whose roots give us the words "Ray" as in "Sun-Ray" as he (Amun-Ra) is a Sun God, or more specifically a "Light" god. Since Mun, is also inclusive of the Moon which also has its rays, often associated with illumination and wisdom. At this time, the Moon represented the physical manifestation of God, and the Sun the spiritual manifestation. The characterisation of the figure in Amun-Ra in Egyptian imagery can be seen with two columns extending from his head, these represent the light or illumination from both the Sun and Moon, he was king of the Gods, and the Astrological pantheons therefore affiliate him with other Sun gods such as Zeus, AKA He-Zeus, spelled Jesus.

On consideration, this is probably why it retained its usage in the later evolution into Christian doctrine. Amun-Ra similarly shares the titles of "the creator", and was the first of the emerging mono-theistic systems in the Egyptian paganistic pantheon that preceded. Coincidentally enough he formed part of a "Holy Trinity" of gods which became the "one in three". The trinity were Amun, Ra and Ptah which represented the Mind, Body and Spirit, similarly to the Father (mind), Son (body) and Holy Ghost (Spirit) comprised the Christian interpretation of this collective.

Ptah is particularly significant in this trinity in that, in Gnosticism he is considered one of the Demiurge, a creator God whose thoughts and words manifest as physical objects and created what we perceive as all reality and the universe. Biblically the significant usage of the word Amen occurs at the end of the New Testament, and thus concluding the "word" and the whole Christian Bible. But it's first occurrence is in the OT's book of numbers, a purely Hebrew set of rules or book of "Law" as spoken to Moses from "The Lord".

The Lord commands Moses to get rid of the sick and anybody corrupted by the dead, he then goes on to condemn anyone who commits sin, defining due restitution for said sin and how it should be made to the family of he that is wronged, or if the wronged person has no family, to the "Kohen" translated in Bible as "priest", while really it means it means "leader", and although it could be argued that "leaders" then were either kingly in status or religious, similarly though they were shamanistic or "wise-ones" which we know as "Wizards". But most interestingly, *The Book of Numbers*, specifically before the use of the word "Amen", describes a spell of divination and curse to be performed by a Kohen to detect if a woman is guilty of being unfaithful to her husband. The spell cast commands, that should she be guilty of being unfaithful to her husband that her thighs shall waste away, and her stomach shall swell, replicating the effect of malnutrition. Signifying that even back then it was used in spell craft, not prayer.

The original "Priests" of the Old-Testament, which you must remember was long before the times of Christ were without exception priests of Baal and Dagon, both of which are now completely aligned with what we call satanic gods or demons. In fact where the OT uses the word "Lord", they are usually referring to Baal in most cases which was again a Sun god, defined by the Astrological Aeon they were in, a concept that although ignored stands to this day. Baal was a Bull during the period of Taurus, and Goat during the period of Aries, bringing us full cycle to the opening statement of the sheep following the Shepherd. The God of the Aeon is defined by an astrological age, and was replaced in name on each transition.

The Piscean god followed creating the Christian Pantheon and the New Testament that we are now familiar with. Which is why the Sun(son) God, in the Christian definition is associated with the fish, the Lord became the fish or the fisher of men (Dagon).

We are entering now the Astrological age of Aquarius, the water bearer, or the wave bearer, this I believe is an unavoidable age of enlightenment, which some may term the age of Lucifer, the light bearer, Lucifer is now the Sun(son) of God, which means the physical realm of mankind will belong to hir (some perceive Lucifer in male form, I personally am inclined towards the feminine based on my research) but that's entirely a personal choice, and as far as I can tell insignificant. The spiritual will always remain with the father as God cannot be manifest in the physical.

YOU ARE ONE OF THE FEW WHO HAVE CHOSEN TO REALISE YOUR DIVINITY YOU ARE ONE OF THE FEW WHO ARE SMART ENOUGH TO ASK QUESTIONS YOUR POTENTIAL IS UNLIMITED FROM THIS MOMENT OF SELF REALISATIONI AM BLESSED TO BE WITH YOU

WE ARE THE FUTURE.

Astrological Angelic Aspects

Angels, messengers of God have been imagined by men since he conceived a definition for a god, and by extension God as a holistic universal benefactor. When we pose to imagine angels, we conjure up imagery of Tolkienesque Elves of beauty, but with apollonic stature, grace and virtue. Their wonderment exaggerated with swan like wings and historically, although falling out of favour with modern artistic interpretation is the halo. Seemingly a hovering crown of luminate divinity doesn't suit our 21st Century aesthetic ideals too much.

That aesthetic notion, and our ability to create and drop the physical definition of these iconic figures of Gods personal favour, shows how the definition of such creatures exists now purely within the mind of man; and not defined by actual entities from which we have gained reference.

Those erudite in the subject of angels will know of the Cherubim and the Seraphim are two distinct types of angels, forming aspects of responsibility in their roles under the command of God. Akin to historical concepts of a royal court, the Cherubim like foot soldiers guard the entrance of paradise. Mentioned in the bible at the point of man's fall from grace, Adam is cast out of Eden, and was prevented from return because the Cherubim were appointed as sentinels to ensuring Adam and his sons (us) would never return into the Garden.

Gen 3:24 "After he drove the man out, he placed on the east side of the Garden of Eden cherubim and a flaming sword flashing back and forth to guard the way to the tree of life."

This is 'The Fall' a seminal moment in the genesis version of the condition of man today, unrecoverably answerable for the failings of our biblical common ancestor. The story, is not that distant from that of the fall of Lucifer, defying God's law he too is banished from a concept of God's grace. His sin, pride; man's sin, rejecting ignorance. Both are a rejection of God's will. A Jealous and Harsh ancient version of God, who seems to have mellowed in his old age. Historically tasting a fruit would get you banished from his blessings, now seemingly, we just have to ask for forgiveness through Jesus Christ and the Flaming sword and Cherubim will move out of the way paving our road with rose petals towards the pearly gates, where St. Peter will be waiting to open them up for us.

The Seraphim, are quite different and not being Aesthetically pleasing to modern art rarely get depicted. Awkwardly they have six wings, two which cover their eyes, two which cover their feet and two which, are to aid their strict obedience to Gods command. No mention of a halo yet exists in terms of angels. But, the seraphim are loyal servants who spend their time eternally praising God. Now the eyes and feet, have great significance in Gnostic concepts, so that in my mind is undoubtedly the purpose of their mention in Isaiah 6. Above him were seraphim, each with six wings: With two wings they covered their faces, with two they covered their feet, and with two they were flying. And they were calling to one another: "Holy, holy, holy is the Lord Almighty; the whole earth is full of his glory."

In Gnostic terms, the eyes represented here are like the proverbial windows to the soul are recipients of light, wisdom and illumination, a trait of the divine and spiritual aspect of man. The feet, touch the earth, they are representative of the physical nature of man. This concept is essential in understanding Hermetic Gnosticism. All things are divided into the above, spiritual nature and the below, physical nature and the holistic which is all between the two. If you look out for these concepts while reading any scripture you will see how important this concept is.

Symbolically the seraphim, cover their eyes so that they do not imitated Lucifer, the light bringer, they are not seeking pride, or wisdom, they avert their eyes in the glory of the light of God. God in biblical terms is "The Sun", or rather iconified As the sun, a source of light. They cover their feet, to renounce the opposing servitude to the nature of the physical. Man ate of the fruit, he indulged in physical and carnal state, the adversary of the spirit, thus satanic aspects of all things which we consider physics.

Many people misconceive the notion of Sun worship, believing it to be simply the worship of that huge glowing sphere in the sky (sol). Practical people will dismiss the notion of any version of Sun worship as now being outdated by our scientific understanding of the Sun and its purpose and function, and in a very superficial sense it is.

But, Solar worship is much greater than that. Sol worship sees the sun not just as an independent star undergoing a relentless nuclear chain reaction that has a life span according to its size fuel, but as iconic of a benefactor universal god, life giving, light giving divine entity.

It is not the worship as the sun being the extent of that entity. The sun merely is a physical manifestation of an all God in our three-dimensional plane of existence and that all suns defy physics and are representations of that one God in space and time. It's a metaphysical outpouring of energy from the source.

In modern day terms, you could consider it like interacting with a live stream of a YouTube vlogger. there is one vlogger, who technically exists outside our immediate dimensions. He has a continually running image which is seen on our home computers or TV all over the world. In a way, we are seeing him live, but in reality, what we are seeing is a representation channel through which we interact, what is actually present on our home computers is a representation and the real Vlogger exists in an alternate location. The Sun forms a portal, or a network link to that pure essence of God. So, sun worship, has never really been about worship the Sun, it is more Worshiping towards the Suna as a symbol, in the same way people pray towards a cross. That fire essence is similar to the essence of summoning the eternal fire within one's self, both aspects are comparable.

Archangels, you may be surprised to learn that Biblically there is only one Archangel. Michael, A Hebrew word which means 'he who life gives' using the truest definition of a messenger of a holistic god is a medium of expression. The message written is done by astrology, the word Astrology means the "Gods writing in the stars". Astro meaning stars and logy, which commonly is related to "logs" and "Logos", which originally meant "god's word". Indeed, that is what the concept of God's word was intended as. An "All" object which manifests itself outside of us, and is present in all things. Often the Bible and preachers will iterate passages of knowledge suggesting God is everywhere. We in a perversion of literacy perceive this as a spirit, entering and observing things.

But, in reality it is quite a modern interpretation to that "All". If you picture all, time and space as being a simplified "all", and the consciousness within each of us being an individual portion of that collective all, whom amongst ourselves combine to make the consciousness of an overriding "all". And, if we exist within that thing, then god per-se cannot present himself to us in the abstract except by iconic representation.

Picture yourself in that classic eighties Dennis Quaid film "Inner Space" where men were miniaturized and then injected inside another person, or if my reference is too old for you, there was an episode of "Rick and Morty" where they when to a funfair in a man's stomach. This man they were in represents the extent of the universe, all things within him are a part of him. So, when a priest answers your question of "show me proof of god", and he replies, "god is in all things" that is what is meant by the original principle. It may come across as wishy-washy avoidance answers. but it really is meant by Hermetic Gnostic teachings that way, it's probable that the person quoting it from the bible doesn't truly understand the metaphysical nature of the response and as the gullible do, will repeat their truth, without truly understanding what they say.

I Saclas

I Saclas place myself in guise of the fool, wilfully I fall upon my sword, as your savoir falls from grace.

It was upon this day in the sixteenth year of the new millennia that I hold as my third and final incarnation to this mortal realm before I ascend high into the depths and low before the heavens.

The Fool, let me assure you is the wisest of all three of my faces. He burdens his ridicule, and laughs half-notioned aspirations of climbing heaven bound. Verily all towers are surely confounded by the reach of the skies and the fortification shouldered under the foundations they rest upon. For I am he that you stand upon to ascend.

As Lord, I am the spirit of sky, I am firmament of foundations and the life water betwixt. For all that lies between is by my law I am master of all that matter.

Of my first incarnation, I was the sour master, all powerful. Tolerance never betide those who dare test me. Wantonly I dispatch mine enemies with vengeful wrath, dare not stand before me heads raised, for they are daisies, spring for the picking, my number was only as the Sun, and I led those who herald my glory

In my second, I was the inheritor, the meek, and I was the godly who bowed before those men who dared to stand, brave they were. My number was many and I followed the one I once was. Servant to the serpent, the number was I of the stars which follow the eternal Baal through his daily journeys. Weak in strength, powerful in weight. force compels my will, like the grave it calls ever down, down, down.

In my third, I was the observer, the all and without number. And now, at last I morphose the fool, I stand and hold both ends of my sword, stand neither servant or master. Oh how I look foolish. "He knows not how to bear arms!" they mock, and laugh.

But I hold both blade and hilt with cause, ally to the defenceless and foe to the wicked. The wisean silently stand and hold the sword at both ends. the unwise think we fools.

If I was wisean, I think I would hide wisdom in parables, lo how the meat be picked apart but rarely gorged upon when shrouded in off.

If I was unwisean, I would again hide my insophis in further parables, to be devoured, but rarely refined. The fool observes the wise starve and the unwise gourmand on parables of truth and profane with equal measure.

Born of rape the horned one's fire rose from the earth I saw the lich bound by his stave, and begat the woman of man for Eveleth shall be Mother of man. And Leviathan the father, mark well these words. All humbled before Bel Nimrods Fire.

nisi priús cum matre suá, sororis, et filiá, rem habuerit.

I am father of Adam, I stand before woman, prone. Her fire drawn to my dry wood does quench my lust. Such fire does burn and the bush must burn to create my offspring eternal.

Beware that third messiah, oh logos of the dead king, he teaches only life in death. I bring the jovial of life. the child of god is man. brought forth in carnality and feast, without which all is inert. Desire and feast, for you will starve eternal.

Saclas the Fool

Evocation of Choronzon

The great beast himself suggests caution when working with Choronzon, the dweller in the Abyss, which was depicted by the classic magicians themselves by Edward Kelly and John Dee. But who is Choronzon?

Within us all Choronzon is our enemy, he truly is a satanic force that opposes our truest self. He expresses himself as inhibition, fear. He is the mask master and creator of your presented self to be shy and respectful of your surroundings. He is inward intimidation, fear of failure, self-doubter and risk assessor.

Often aspects are portrayed on a somewhat envious sense, a sin or a desire that our carnal self would indulge in if we were not bound and gagged by a self-imposed code of conduct. Despite our heavily endorsed rejection of "ego" in the which is prevalent in the Luciferian community, and not one I personally endorse, we massage our ego to fit in to society, we like to be liked, we wear our mask according to our immediate social environment.

Choronzon tricks us into believing that these "morals" are a productive and worthwhile endeavour. He is evil who portrays himself as good and if you ever want to know the devil, know that he is a trickster, he will never lie with you when he can lie to you.

If you think about the absolute disposal of all inhibitions and morals, doing exactly what we want, when we want and consider it as the ultimate expression of the free will. The free will we are granted as a sentient being. No laws, moral guidance or taboo would be excluded from us. Murder, rape, incest, gluttony, homosexuality, drug use, alcohol, masturbation, bestiality, indiscriminate destruction of life and of society, racism, genocide would all be within our remit as a form of personal expression without remorse, guilt or even apprehension.

I am not being a homophobe myself by listing homosexuality as "taboo" there, but I list it to point out that while I fully endorse this as a right in society today my *personal moral hang-up* would not allow me to engage in same gender sexual activity. But for those of you that would, I was not born that way and I should not take shame in it any more than you should. I do actually envy your nearer step to liberation than I have achieved, but then the question arises "is it an expression of liberation if you are naturally inclined?".

You cannot fight nature, and you should not. I support you wholeheartedly and I'm trying to explain social morals which extended as I typed into personal ones, and I feel I should as always be honest in the subject throughout.

We effectively condition ourselves into believing that our higher moral purpose is to our betterment, but subjectively select our morals to suit our lifestyle, drug users will justify their actions, none drug users will be complacent or feel morally superior to those that do indulge.

Our higher self is ingratiated and by taking this moral high ground we likewise seek to ingratiate ourselves to society. This is still a massage of personal ego, no matter how hard a Luciferian such as myself will boast about his rejection of the ego. Ironically I find a lot of Luciferians who massage their ego by telling you of their superiority to you by the extent of the rejection of their ego.

And I'm as guilty as everyone else, it's not a criticism of my brothers, just an observation we all need to repeatedly reflect upon. Look within to accept its bearing or deny it and do not benefit from its truth.

By weakening your resolve Choronzon, places these doubts of self within our minds. Do we truly reject heinous acts in ourselves and in others because we believe it makes us better people, or because we fear societal repercussions?

This is not just in law, but in how our contemporaries perceive us. We seek social integration through mutual endorsement.

We seek each other out in social groups then when we find "like minded" individuals we seek ways to tell them how wrong they are in their ideals. A moral superiority battle ensues while the liberal minded try to ascend apotheosis of being the most liberal of liberal. To the point where anyone who is not as liberal minded as they, should be shot!

This is the bitter sweet law of Choronzon. And an aspect used by your manipulators to imprison you.

You can be sure as hell, if someone wants to remove your freedoms they will start by selling you an ideal of greater freedom.

"Why should you walk in fear of people carrying a pineapple, we shall ensure that your freedom is protected by banning people carrying pineapples"

But before they make such claims you will be inundated with "pineapple horror" stories.

This technique is used everywhere in our 21st century.

Apply the above code of "pineapple" to guns, Muslims, mobile phones, internet free speech, "fake news". You can be certain that anything you have come to despise, it is Choronzonic example of trickery.

For better or for worse be the end results, be sure that you recognise the trickery being cast upon you.

Choronzon produces his results by complete opposition to expected desire, and that is how he is master of deception and a dangerous entity to work with.

Choronzon is an example of giving people enough rope to hang themselves with. If you wander the desert dying of thirst, and pray for water, beware the flood that drowns you. He is the divine comedy which makes all things that are delicious to the taste, the very things that are worst for your health.

The point I'm trying to make about Choronzon is that you will never succeed in taking advantage of him, the best you can do is recognise him and ride the disturbance wave that he presents to you, as it is only through knowing it is his work that you can feast at his table, but know which point to leave the supper.

This is the master/slave relationship described later in this book, there is little difference between the two, only perception.

We believe our morals are exemplary and admirable aspects of our selves, that we choose them and set standards by their presence. In reality Choronzon instructs our moral codes, they become our master, we do not have morals by choice, if they are a choice go ahead…break one! See who is master.

If you do manage to break a personal moral code, you think that it is over? You won? No there is the eternal punishment from Choronzon. He will haunt you, he will present himself in regret and disgust, and he will humiliate you from the inside out and tear you apart.

Guilt, nauseous disappointment in the very self for taking mastery of the self.

Choronzon, works through you, he is always present, and is indeed a very powerful force. To work with Choronzon, you really need to recognise what aspects of you he masters already. The best you can do is to push him out, rather than call him in. There is very little advantage to you to introduce Choronzon into further aspects, he is best user with evocation rather than invocation.

Even seeking Choronzon will present himself as an alternative aspect, convincing you that you have failed in your quest, he could even present another as Choronzon. He is the epitome of diabolism.

To find him, you must not seek him and he will always be there. This is why he often falls into the realms of those who practice chaos magic, their remit to invoke magic without intent and see the results is perfect for Choronzon. Empty mediation techniques may result in a Choronzon encounter.

Choronzon is fluidic in his presence, he adapts and is negative to aspiration. So inversion and chaos are his methods. He has no known symbol, this allows him his free supremacy in the nether realms. He has not been pinned, even his name is unknown and varying spellings of Choronzon merely allude to the aspect, not his true self.

We are our own aspect of Choronzon, our many facets mentioned earlier are merely representations of our self, as is Choronzon, he has infinite facets and any he presents to us, may not be presented to anyone else.

He is considered dangerous as by expelling Choronzon from yourself could result in a much-required inhibition being removed. And you certainly should fear your immoral self. Alternatively invoking he, could lead to self-seclusion, extreme inhibitions and acrophobia, or a feeling of all self-worth being vanquished.

Nindaranna, she calls, temptress maiden of perpetual erudition, dawn's succubus of the wisean. She whispers in visions, the consort of spectral union.
Beckon she, my awakening from her throne, set low on the horizon commanding all the seven seas.

The risen whore of Babylon, mother of all fruits yet to delight. Pandora whose gifts throw shadows on all other desire, and hurls the mortal aspirations unto each of seven infinite abysses.

Glorious winds howl her divine melody past my ears, I am awakened by her and she consumes me with no less abandonment than I consume her, fixated I stare, for there is not now, nor ever else a place to look with such equalled adoration.

To know Nindaranna is to one's own heart. She, goddess, is surely more grace to mine eyes than the nectar of love itself, as love can be only made prisoner by my mortal estate, furnished too modest to abode her bountiful volume.
Morn cock crows, and my industry summoned, through drawn curtains I fight the sidereal veil of blinding obfuscation and its confoundment of much which is to be held without regard.

Her Angels from their mountain peaks, harken me "come hither". I abide, for they teach me the dance of each hue, where all become one and one become all, from each vista more is revealed. Each complete themselves, yet none whole without each.

We engage in such passionate bliss that I am not lost or consumed, more, I never was. And always it was we, always we eight, for without my eye their scintillate bodies is naught but unbroken shadow in the unwalled passage of endless light.
I stand atop those mountain peaks, and survey the seas and land before me. A great flood must wash away that embered dust, that nothing remains than my bare feet washed upon Masis.

Behold withdrawn tide which relinquishes new world, I shall claim crown over, my queen forever at my side.

RICHARD K PAGE

Other Books by this Author

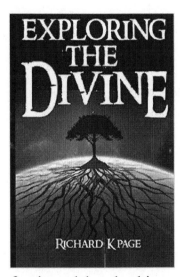

Exploring the Divine

Is a compilation of examinations and theories into the great wonders of the universe and our place in it. It explores God, the creation of the universe, Demons, Angels, Black Holes, Black Magic, the big bang, Origins of religion, possibility of the computer-generated universe, time travel, space exploration, the perception of the self and a universal consciousness. If you are one of those people that is fascinated by the big questions of life, then this book will either provide answers or give you many interesting and new ways of philosophising the great mysteries of the universe. There is not a dull chapter, and there is something for everyone with an inquisitive mind. It also offers an aspect of spiritual guidance for those battling between the evidence of the modern world and reconciliation with biblical texts. The book is split into two distinct halves beginning with religion and following up with scientific theories that are not your run of the mill current thinking but whole new concepts that will provide interesting discussions for yourself and your friends all of which while not proven or supported by current thinking are equally valid and certainly not disproven. An objective view of religion without the purpose of either converting you to a faith or supporting atheism, but redefining our understanding of the God concept in a way compatible with modern physics and the known creation of the universe. The two are not exclusive of each other. Are God and the Devil one and the same? Good and bad, the balance, cycle and flow of universal energy, new wave thought, magic and mysticism. Word origins and meanings. Biblical misinterpretations. A source book for anyone seeking to understand. You cannot come away from this book the same person. Teleportation, the human occupation of distant planets in others star systems all made possible using current technology, evolution vs intelligent design.

£9.99 Paperback

ISBN-10: 1519281854

ISBN-13: 978-1519281852

Product Dimensions: 15.2 x 1.3 x 22.9 cm

⭐⭐⭐⭐⭐ **Exploring the Divine is a good thinking persons book**
By Chris Hill on 25 Feb. 2015

Format: Kindle Edition | Verified Purchase
A very interesting read,Exploring the Divine is a good thinking persons book.
Gets the old grey matter working.
Once I opened it I couldn't put it down.
I cant wait for his next book...

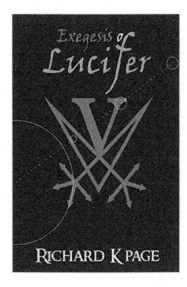

Exegesis of Lucifer

Is an exploration of the Lucifer archetype. Lucifer has and is identified in many cultures, religions and mythos around the world.

Fallen angel, demon, the Devil or Satan himself.

In this book, we compare the gnostic traits of dualism that is present in Luciferian philosophy and compare it to other Gods and Legends with similar traits in the Greek, Arthurian, Egyptian, Nordic and Celtic legends.

As you explore your Luciferian path many people will use comparisons to other archetypes, this one place sourcebook will give you a thorough understanding of these related principles.

- £19.99 Paperback.
- ISBN-10: 1519443153
- ISBN-13: 978-1519443151
- Product Dimensions: 15.2 x 0.9 x 22.9 cm

★★★★★ Expands your mind
By John Black on 27 Jan. 2016

Format: Paperback
Not usually something i would read but I spotted it during my trawling soft the Internet and I have to say, thouroughly enjoyable read. Filled with interesting concepts and ideas that I had never even thought of before.
It was well set out and easy to understand.
All in all a very recommendable book :)

Luciferianism: AlterEgo

This book extols the metamorphosis stage of your path towards apotheosis. Previously my books have explored mythos, archetypes, hidden meanings and principle systems. Finally, AlterEgo is the first book in my series which engages with practices and concepts that can be put to use so that you can to achieve the secrets of absolute material success, expression of free will, achievement of ambitions through a three-pronged attack using Luciferian manipulation of Materialism, Supernaturalism, and Idealism. Now is the time to embrace the change within humanity, break free the shackles of this illusory world and the overthrow the manipulators that bind you into a life of obscurity. Wealth, Power, and Freedom can be directly obtained by the full extent of the power that Luciferian wisdom, magick and ethos can provide. AlterEgo Identifies the artificial obstructions in your life, and the lives of countless other regular human beings, fighting endlessly on this revolving door of just surviving rather than living. It brings you to the realization of who and what are the adversaries that bind you and allows you to destroy their hypnotic influence over you. This program releases the true you, your Lucifer deific alter ego and diminishes the historically reserved you; bound by Morals, Obligations, Social conformity, Guilt, and False Education until now you never stood a chance. Overthrow the tables, the tide has turned, now is your turn to be the morning star, rising above those who claim the throne. This is what

Luciferianism is really about. This book contains realizations, rituals and wisdom rarely discussed. This is the Luciferian book that changes everything for you.

Amazon.com: ⭐⭐⭐⭐⭐ 1 review

1 of 1 people found the following review helpful

⭐⭐⭐⭐⭐ **A++++++++ Two Thumbs Up, with a Cherry on top of a Sundae, or an eye on top of a pyramid ;)** 14 May 2016

By Fallen Angel - **Published on Amazon.com**

Format: Paperback | **Verified Purchase**

A great book that is written professionally and explains, and demonstrates the concepts, ideologies, and principles of Luciferianism. His first two books are a great collection to add; and very inspiring. This third book from him is truly inspiring and enlightening. I learned a lot of information from this book that I did not previously know. I look forward to the fourth book by this author.

⭐⭐⭐⭐⭐ **A must read!!**

By Amazon Customer on 29 July 2016

Format: Paperback | Verified Purchase

An excellent book I definitely recommend reading. Down to earth, yet an eye opening account, written in layman's terms, in such a way that even if you are new to Luciferian philosophy or the corruption at Elite levels, this book illustrates, beautifully with its words, a true account of the content. I couldn't put it down once I'd started and will be searching out the other books by Richard K Page. Deserves to be a best seller. If everyone could spare a day to reading it, the world would be a better place and this you will understand if you read it. Certainly 5 stars and more from me!

- £9.99 Paperback
- ISBN-10: 1530881773
- ISBN-13: 978-1530881772
- Product Dimensions: 15.2 x 1.1 x 22.9 cm

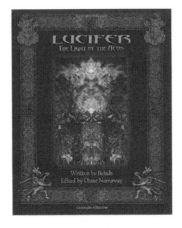

Lucifer: The Light of The Aeon.

One of the Rebels that contributed to this amazon best selling Occult genre book.

A unique collection of articles, poems, and art contributed by different authors and artists, all of which work with and approach Lucifer subjectively; giving the reader a greater range of information and with it a deeper understanding of Lucifer from the heart of the Luciferian.

Lucifer: The Light of the Aeon Paperback – 2 Sep 2016
by Diane Narraway ▾ (Author), Teach Carter (Author), Jaclyn Cherie ▾ (Author), Elizabeth Jennings (Author), Rachel Summers (Author), Geraldine Lambert (Author), Einwen Morgan (Author), Richard K. Page ▾ (Author), Laurie Pneumatikos ▾ (Author), Cheryl Waldron (Author), Sean Witt ▾ (Author)
★★★★★ ▾ 8 customer reviews

- £19.30 Paperback
- ISBN-10: 1890399523
- ISBN-13: 978-1890399528
- Product Dimensions: 20.3 x 1.9 x 25.4 cm

★★★★★ **Brilliant**
By Rune K on 19 Oct. 2016

Format: Paperback

This is a brilliant book. I have learned quite a lot from it. Things I can use and return to as serious inspirational, wonderful stuff. Self-awareness is a keyword here. Individuality is another. The destruction of the too often sought consensus, that makes everything seem less magic and more easily corrupted by hijacked language because it disintegrates the potential and possibilities in transformational solitary power. There are many interpretations in the book to reflect upon and as with any good book it opens up for the urge to further study the subjects in it. There are passages in it that are very autobiographical, others focus on different rituals and others again talk in depth about mythology, possible connections and openness concerning the doubts linked to these. There is not the slightest hint of being dictated anything which is always annoying. Instead there is a celebration of being a rebel in a way that creates challenges and with those challenges makes important moves in life, in society through inner worlds approached with honesty and courage. The solitary aspect which is very present in a lot of the contributions speaks directly to me. It says in my experience don't let anyone else hijack the language of your life, your life IS your language. It is a real celebration of freedom, of constantly working with freeing, acknowledging change as a fundamental process in life. All the contributions are written with great clarity which is surprising in itself. The many voices create a very dynamic collection. Another book in my collection now that I will return to once in a while to remember the strength of it. Of course, I highly recommend it.

Comment | One person found this helpful. Was this review helpful to you? | Yes | No | Report abuse

★★★★★ **like a glimpse inside the writers lives and into their ...**
By Mrs Rebecca Holder on 5 Dec. 2016

Format: Paperback | Verified Purchase

A really enlightening book. like a glimpse inside the writers lives and into their souls.... Highly recommend this book, I'm a complete novice when it comes to information about Lucifer but this is fascinating. I have a short attention span at the minute, but I have dipped in and out, reading my favourite authors first, returning to sections to re read them with growing enlightenment. A really lovely book to hold, look at and, as my dear old headmistress used to say, read, mark, learn and inwardly digest...

Comment | One person found this helpful. Was this review helpful to you? | Yes | No | Report abuse

★★★★★ **its approach reads like someone telling you how it is**
By Amazon Customer on 18 Sept. 2016

Format: Paperback | Verified Purchase

This book's originality lies in the fact that it is so subjective, borne of the individual experiences of those included but this, in my opinion, is no ordinary anthology. This book leaves nothing set in stone and left me rather breathless as to its scope; its approach reads like someone telling you how it is, or how it has always been for them as individuals with each their own unique take on this complicated but essential character - Lucifer. More than that, each and every contributor is that few degrees closer to you they are that tangible.

It bleeds as much as it wears its heart on its sleeve., complete with an absence of dogma and its beauty owes as much to a fluid read as it does the originality of each approach to Lucifer, as it does the style of each author. There is a great poetry in some of the prose and I cannot underestimate the primacy of the subjective approach here, it is that personal. Not only have I – the reader - learnt but felt.

I can only hail those involved for the illumination they have made real into words but be prepared...this may make you question everything, challenge and ask you where you stand. In places you may put this book down for the emotions evoked and the tears that lead all the way down the rays of light into that very personal, powerful truth...

Available in all good book stores and solophi.com

Made in the USA
Columbia, SC
11 November 2022

70907064R00093